K9 OBEDIENCE TRAINING

K9 Professional Training Series

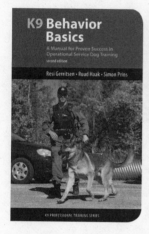

K9 Behavior Basics
A Manual for Proven Success in Operational Service Dog Training
second edition
Resi Gerritsen • Ruud Haak • Simon Prins
K9 PROFESSIONAL TRAINING SERIES

K9 Drug Detection
A Manual for Training and Operations
Resi Gerritsen • Ruud Haak
K9 PROFESSIONAL TRAINING SERIES

K9 Line-up Training
A Manual for Suspect Identification and Detection Work
Resi Gerritsen • Ruud Haak • Simon Prins
K9 PROFESSIONAL TRAINING SERIES

K9 Professional Tracking
A Complete Manual for Theory and Training in Clean-Scent Tracking
second edition
Resi Gerritsen • Ruud Haak
K9 PROFESSIONAL TRAINING SERIES

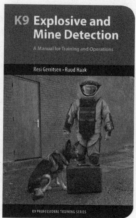

K9 Explosive and Mine Detection
A Manual for Training and Operations
Resi Gerritsen • Ruud Haak
K9 PROFESSIONAL TRAINING SERIES

K9 Schutzhund Training
A Manual for IGP Training through Positive Reinforcement
Updated second edition
Resi Gerritsen • Ruud Haak
K9 PROFESSIONAL TRAINING SERIES

See the complete list at
dogtrainingpress.com

K9 OBEDIENCE TRAINING

Teaching Pets and Working Dogs to Be Reliable and Free-Thinking

Susan Bulanda

K9 Professional Training Series

An imprint of
Brush Education Inc.

23 24 25 6 5 4 3

Brush Education Inc.
www.brusheducation.ca
contact@brusheducation.ca

Cover design: John Luckhurst; Cover image: Susan Bulanda
Interior design: Carol Dragich, Dragich Design

Printed and manufactured in Canada

Library and Archives Canada Cataloguing in Publication
Title: K9 obedience training : teaching pets and working dogs to be reliable
    and free-thinking /Susan Bulanda.
Names: Bulanda, Susan, author.
Description: Series statement: K9 professional training series
Identifiers: Canadiana (print) 20190076836 | Canadiana (ebook) 20190076895 |
    ISBN 9781550597912 (softcover) | ISBN 9781550597929 (PDF) |
    ISBN 9781550597936 (Kindle) | ISBN 9781550597943 (EPUB)
Subjects: LCSH: Dogs—Training—Handbooks, manuals, etc. |
    LCSH: Working dogs—Training—Handbooks, manuals, etc. |
    LCSH: Dogs—Behavior. | LCSH: Working dogs—Behavior.
Classification: LCC SF431 .B85 2019 | DDC 636.7/0835—dc23

Dedication

I want to dedicate this book to my very dear and good friend Dan Guin. He started as an old-fashioned dog trainer and had the wisdom to change to positive training methods. He attended both of my programs at Kutztown University and came with me on most of my consults. His understanding of canine nature and behavior has been a real asset for me. He will be dearly missed.

Dan Guin
1937–2018

Contents

PART III: BASIC OBEDIENCE TRAINING

Acknowledgments

I want to thank Tom Lore, Meaghan Craven, Kay Rollans, John Luckhurst, Carol Dragich, and Lauri Seidlitz from Brush Education Inc. for all of their help on this book and on *K9 Search and Rescue Troubleshooting*, my previous book. They are an excellent team, making the publication of both books an enjoyable experience. I also want to thank Kathy Montgomery for reading the rough draft of this book and for posing for some of the photos. Vi Hummel Shaffer also deserves a thanks for proofreading this manuscript and giving me helpful input. Last but not least, I want to thank Matt and Jade Madairy and their dog Grady, as well as Kevin and Ginger Bronke and their dog Sunny, for being the subjects of many of the photos in this book.

Foreword

Your dog depends on you for his safety and well-being, and the best way to ensure this is through good communication that is grounded in solid obedience training. *K9 Obedience Training: Teaching Pets and Working Dogs to Be Reliable and Free-Thinking* is aimed at providing the best foundational obedience training for future working dogs and their handlers who will go beyond basic obedience to specialized training. That being said, it is also the best guide for domestic dogs (whether they be puppies or wise, old veterans) and their dog-loving owners, and for anyone considering getting a dog. Sue's knowledge, skills, and internationally recognized expertise come from years of training and handling working dogs, including search and rescue (SAR) dogs, sled dogs, and "problem" dogs (and people). Her philosophy is based on communication and a positive training method—that is, a method that focuses on positive reinforcement rather than negative, punishment-based communication. What makes *K9 Obedience Training* special is that it explains what to do, what not to do, and, most importantly, *why*.

Sue details how to communicate with your dog and lays out the necessary steps for successful obedience training. The book explains, for example, that you must choose specific words for specific commands—and commit to their consistent use—before trying to teach them to your dog. She further explains teaching tools, offers excellent tips and exercises, and discusses some of the differences between these and other dog training methods. She outlines common mistakes and basic issues that dog trainers, handlers, and owners make, and how to avoid them. What's more, Sue lets us in on how ours dogs themselves think about and understand training.

It is critical to understand that you have a *thinking* dog—so you ought to be a thinking owner. *You* must clearly understand the behaviors and skills that you want to train before you teach them to your dog, and you must think about how *your dog* thinks in order to avoid miscommunication. Human language is a foreign language to a dog. They don't understand it the way we do; rather, for a dog that *has* learned to recognize a human word, that word will be linked to a very specific action or object, and *only* to that action or object. Your dog will not understand you if you use synonyms, or if you use a particular word in a new way that the dog has not been trained to understand—and this can be frustrating for both you and your dog. Try putting yourself in your dog's position:

OWNER: Bruno!! How many times have I told you to STAY OFF the COUCH!? This is expensive furniture!

BRUNO: *Wait—how do I STAY and OFF at the same time? Maybe I can OFF my back feet to the floor and STAY my front feet on the ... Hey—you said STAY OFF the COUCH. I'm on the comfy CHAIR. You never said, "Chair." By the way, what is "furniture?"*

It is, therefore, very important to learn to think like your dog: work on one command at a time and show your dog the connection between the command word and the desired action. But it is also important to note that, although dogs learn to understand human words in very precise ways, context *does* matter—and we should always remember that although dogs understand our language *differently* than we do, they are not stupid. Far from it! Dogs are entirely capable of learning different sets of rules for different situations and with different people. They can learn just about anything as long as you can show them clearly what you want, one step at a time.

I don't just write this out of hearsay, but out of experience. I completed Sue's Canine Training and Management program at college, and now work as a dog sitter at what I call "dog camp." Using Sue's method, I have trained the dogs that I watch to respond to rules and commands that may be totally different than those established at their homes. Upon arriving at camp, they race through the house, sniffing everything at nose level to make sure nothing has changed. Then they check the toy basket, make sure the camp cats are around, and jump up on the couch or bed, wriggling around until they are stretched out, belly up (something many are not allowed to do at home, although they may try it once or twice after camp to see if home rules have changed to match camp rules!). At camp, the dogs know that *bedtime* means piling up on the bed, getting a treat, and settling down to sleep. They know *good morning* means they can start bouncing on the bed without being corrected. They know the word *togofer* and respond to it by freezing in place, waiting to hear what follows: "Do you want ... (*dramatic pause*) togofer ... a ... walk?" And when I say, "Let's go feed the kitties," they race down the basement stairs to the cats' feeding station.

This book gives you clear, straightforward exercises and explanations to help you and your dog through the process of developing solid obedience training that makes sense to both of you. Along the way, it will open your eyes to the intelligence and flexibility of the canine intellect in many contexts. Get ready to be amazed by your canine and *read this book!*

Kathy Montgomery

Kathy Montgomery has been a dog sitter
for the past 25 years, both in boarding
kennel and dog camp contexts.

Introduction

Learning from Dogs: How I Became a Free-Thinking Dog Trainer

I started training my own dogs when I was in grammar school. My first purebred dog was a Collie named Lassie. I was about 10 years old when we got her. Unbeknownst to my family she was deaf—but I was still able to teach her obedience and tricks.

Lassie would often get underfoot and we would step on her paw. Each time we did this we would get down next to her and rub her paw saying, "Oh poor Lassie, I'm sorry." After a while, she started to limp rather frequently, holding one front foot off the floor, even when no one had stepped on her foot. After a while (and after determining that she was not, in fact, hurt), we realized that she had learned to limp in order to get us to rub her foot!

Shortly after this, we would learn that Lassie's habit of getting underfoot was due to the fact that she was deaf. A deaf dog can be a challenge, but since I was born hearing impaired, I understood deafness, and my training with her got much better.

We talk a lot, in dog training, about how to produce and reproduce certain behaviors in the dog; but what we don't talk about is how the dog is capable of doing the same thing in us. Lassie's

Photo 0.1 Lassie, my deaf dog.

limping trick was just this: an astute perception of the facts of her world, of the emotional responses of the people in it, and of her desire to have *us* do something for *her*. Lassie opened my eyes to the tremendous capacity dogs have to be creative, playful, clever, observant, even manipulative—in a word, intelligent. I was lucky to have, as my first dog, not just a pet, but an *individual*. She was not only a sharp learner who easily picked up on what I had to teach, but also an exquisite teacher. She taught me, on many occasions, what *she* could do, and what she thought about the world. Lassie was my introduction to free-thinking dogs, the first in what has turned out to be a long line.

By the time I was in ninth grade—a few years after these first experiences with Lassie—I had earned a reputation as a dog trainer and was asked if my dog and I would perform in the ninth-grade talent show. My dog at the time was Pal, a German Shepherd/ Collie mix. He had already been in local dog shows doing his tricks, and I knew he was able to perform in front of an audience. In fact, Pal *loved* to perform—he was also a real ham. So, of course, I agreed to be in the talent show.

Pal's routine for the show was to jump through a paper-covered hoop, go up and down a special ladder with steps on both sides, and then bark in time with "How Much Is That Doggie in the Window." The last trick worked like this: I had trained Pal to bark when I raised the pinky of my right hand, and to stop barking when I lowered it. Another student played the tune on the piano, pausing at certain moments in the song. In these moments, I would raise my right pinky, Pal would bark twice, I would lower my pinky, and the song would continue. I told the student not to continue playing until Pal barked twice. We had rehearsed this act a number of times in the school auditorium with absolutely no problems, and I felt confident it would go over well.

The day of the talent show came, and it was my turn to go on stage. Pal was off-leash since he was well trained. My props were already set up. The first act was to jump through the hoop. I sent Pal to the end of the stage and gave him the command, "Through the hoop!" He ran across the stage at full speed and then ... went *under* the hoop. The audience roared with laughter. He had never done that before. I was not sure what to do and was embarrassed beyond words. I told Pal, "Go back and do it again." He went back to the end of the stage and I re-commanded him, "Through the hoop!" Pal looked at me, looked at the audience and sauntered across the stage while looking at the audience, walked up to the hoop, looked at it and then leaped through it. Again, the audience went crazy clapping.

Next, he had to climb the ladder. He did that almost as he should, with the exception that he paused at the top, just looking out at the audience—I swear I saw him stick out his chest!—before going down the other side. I was relieved, feeling the routine could yet be saved, if we could just get through the song without a hitch.

Pal and I walked across the stage and stood near the piano, just as we had rehearsed. The student started playing and, at the first pause in the music, I raised my finger. Pal barked twice, I lowered my finger, and the music continued. At the next pause in the song, I raised my pinky finger and Pal only barked once. Everything stopped: since I had told the student not to continue until he heard two barks, the music didn't pick up again. What to do? I raised my pinky again—no bark. (How forcefully can you raise a pinky?) Finally, after what seemed like forever, I simply said, "Pal, where is the other bark!?" Pal took a good look at

Photo 0.2 Pal, the ham.

me—and that brat barked one more time! The audience roared and clapped. I died. Everyone thought that I had taught Pal to be a comedian, but the fact is he did it on his own—like Lassie, he thought for himself.

I learned a lot from my early dog training escapades and have continued to learn through the years. Perhaps most of all, I've learned never to underestimate the capacity of dogs to think for themselves, and always to be open to the contributions that your dog makes in your relationship.

Early in my career, while at an obedience trial, I watched a man compete with his German Shepherd Dog. When he called his dog on the recall, the dog came—but he came with his head and tail down, almost slinking. A product of the jerk-and-hurt training method that was common at the time, this dog could obey, but he wasn't having fun. This was obvious to anyone watching, and it was heartbreaking. I decided, right then and there, that I would develop a new training method: one that didn't just work, but that dogs loved. One that took dogs' emotional well-being seriously and understood their mind and their feelings to be central to successful training. My motto became, "Dogs will come with their heads up and their tails wagging."

I have been training dogs professionally since about 1961, first as a dog trainer, then working in search and rescue (SAR) and as a certified canine/feline behavior consultant with the International Association of Animal Behavior Consultants. I have also trained and competed with dogs in obedience and conformation. Each experience in these venues has taught me new aspects of the canine mind and new dimensions of dogs' abilities that have both helped me develop my training methods and bolstered my commitment to the principle behind these methods: that dogs' ability to feel and to think for themselves should be front-and-center in any training program.

Over the course of my career, I have seen training methods and our understanding of the dog's mind evolve dramatically in ways that confirm and deepen some of my early intuitions about dogs— that they are intelligent, emotional beings, like us. And yet, despite these advances, when it comes to obedience, it seems that many dog trainers still cannot handle the concept of a free-thinking dog. They want, instead, a robotically obedient dog. In my opinion, this is not conducive to the dog's mental well-being (nor, it should be noted, his physical well-being since, like us, a dog's mental and physical health are linked). For this reason, I felt that a canine obedience training book that emphasizes positive training methods and encourages dogs to be free-thinking was needed. This is that book.

A Breakdown of the Book

The pages that follow are a reflection of the training philosophy I've been developing since the beginning of my career. It has been shaped by the dogs I have worked with who have taught me again and again what it is to be a dog that thinks freely.

The book is divided into three parts. In Part I, I set the stage by outlining some of the central concepts behind my training philosophy. Chapter 1 deals with the concept of the "free-thinking dog," while Chapter 2 unpacks the central ideas that make up my positive training philosophy.

Before you begin training your dog, it is important for the free-thinking dog trainer to understand some basic guidelines and skills, and this can be found in Part II. Chapter 3 lays out the dos and don'ts of communicating with your dog, explains the signals that dogs most pick up on, and outlines what to be aware of in your communication style in order to avoid miscommunication and confusion. Chapter 4 answers some of the important questions that should be asked before you begin training your dog: Who should train the dog? When should you start? What should your dog be eating? Then, in Chapter 5, we look at effective housetraining and crate training strategies that are safe and healthy for both you and your dog. And finally, Chapter 6 looks at getting your dog used to having his body handled to avoid negative experiences during grooming and vet visits, or other situations in which your dog may be handled. This chapter also gives an overview of basic grooming. Although this book is about teaching basic obedience, you will also learn how to teach your dog skills such as accepting equipment and having his body parts handled. These skills are part of the rules for living, making life easier and less frightening for dogs.

Once you are ready to start training, crack open the book to Part III. Chapter 7 discusses the equipment required for basic obedience training and how to introduce it to your dog, and Chapter 8 goes over how to set up your training schedule and environment for success. My basic obedience program is found in Chapter 9: this is where you will find detailed instructions on positive training methods for basic obedience exercises. Once you and your dog have mastered the exercises in Chapter 9, move on to Chapter 10 for more advanced exercises. Chapter 11 provides a few exercises for preventing (or, if required, correcting) common problematic behaviors such as jumping up on people and excessive barking and chewing. Finally, Chapter 12 goes over some simple tricks to teach your dog, and serves as a reminder that it's always important to mix work with fun. Obedience training is no exception.

The basic training methods and exercises in the book are ideal for the working dog, a dog that must think on his own in various situations that cannot be duplicated in training. The advice provided here is not meant to give you a robotically obedient dog, but a dog that is well-behaved, keen to work with you, and able to enjoy life to the fullest. To that extent, it will also be a valuable text for the pet dog owner. Whatever your situation, it is my hope that you will be able to benefit from my years of experience training dogs to think freely.

DISCLAIMER

While the contents of this book are based on substantial experience and expertise, working with dogs involves inherent risks, especially in dangerous settings and situations. Anyone using approaches described in this book does so entirely at their own risk and both the author and publisher disclaim any liability for any injuries or other damage that may be sustained.

Part I

Training Your Dog
to Think Freely

1

What Is a Free-Thinking Dog?

What is a free-thinking dog? In short, it is a dog that can think for himself. This is a dog that will invent games on his own or solve novel problems, doing things and making connections between events and objects that he was never explicitly taught. You may have already met or even owned a free-thinking dog. These dogs are often fun dogs to spend time with, providing lots of laughs with their antics, and tending to be more confident, cool, and collected in the face of new or difficult situations.

Whether or not you've met a free-thinking dog, it is important to remember that all dogs do *think*—there is no question about that. Although it is true that some breeds are bred specifically to think on their own, and that certain individual dogs will be more inclined to think freely than others, the ability of a dog to think freely (or not) is, more often than not, more dependent on the dog's training than on his breed. That is, free thinking is something that can be actively taught—or not—in training. This means that, by using the correct methods, a dog can become more able to think and act reliably and independently. This is a necessary skill for the working dog, who will often find himself faced with novel problems and situations that cannot be specifically trained.

Not all training methods encourage free thinking in the dog. Specifically, methods that require exact responses from the dog and correct every deviation from the desired behavior tend to discourage free thought. When a dog is not encouraged to think freely, the dog becomes hesitant to do anything other than what he is told to do. The dog will not think on his own or make decisions, even if he is given a command that puts him in an uncomfortable or even dangerous situation. For example—and I have seen this happen—if an owner commands his dog to "Down-stay" in the direct sun, the dog down-stays, no questions asked, even if he's uncomfortable, and even if there is shade a few feet away. Those are the rules. Again, while some dogs may behave this way because of their individual personality—they are not inclined to think for themselves—this is most often a learned behavior.

A free-thinking dog in the same situation might make a slightly different choice. He will still follow the command, but might play with the rules. For instance, he might get up, move to the shade, and then do his down-stay. This kind of playing with rules differs from both the stiff following of rules described above and from *breaking* the rules, or simply not obeying. A dog that is breaking the rules will simply not do what he was asked to do, perhaps because he doesn't have the self-control to obey the command. A free-thinking dog, on the other hand, *will* obey the command in a way that is both comfortable and safe for him.

The Free-Thinking Dog at Work

When a dog struggles to think freely, he may not be successful in a working context. Take this example: we once had a handler and her very nice, champion obedience dog come to our unit. The handler wanted to train her dog in SAR. This dog seemed to have all the qualifications of a good SAR dog. She was friendly, pleasant, good with people, very intelligent, and physically fit. However, in order to win the highest level of obedience competition, she was taught to do what she was told, when she was told, and precisely in the way she was taught. Her training did not allow her to deviate from her routines.

We started with one of the most basic SAR training exercises, in which the handler hides from the dog, who is then meant to find her. The dog typically gets very excited and wants to find the handler, his owner. This dog showed real promise: she got very excited, had a good nose, and was able to run right to the handler. She really got into this "find the person" game, so much so that she momentarily forgot her obedience training and was able to simply play.

In the next round of training, a volunteer ran and hid for the handler and dog to find. At first, the dog did well. She did succeed in finding the hidden volunteer. However, after she found the volunteer, you could see her whole demeanor change: she went into obedience mode, losing the excitement of the game and replacing it instead with the resolution that she must wait for the next command. Nothing we did could get her to think on her own. All the members of the unit saw this, even the dog's owner, and we all knew that the dog would progress no further in her SAR training. This was unfortunately due to her previous training, which never allowed her to do anything but what she was told, and had diminished her ability to think freely. This dog failed at her SAR training because in some contexts, including SAR, a dog must be free-thinking in order to do a job or complete a task well—must, that is, be able to act on her own, without needing to be told what to do every step of the way.

In the context of SAR, a dog that knows that his handler is wrong or has missed something *must* disobey in order to show the handler what he has found: a clue, maybe, or a related object, or even the missing person. An experienced handler will learn to trust his dog, but almost every handler fails to do this at one time or another. I am no exception. Once, when one of my SAR dogs,

Scout, was young and not very experienced, I sent him by an over-hanging bank of a river to check if a missing person's body was caught underwater in the roots of the trees. He came back and gave me the signal that nothing was there. I thought he worked too fast, so I sent him out again. The second time he worked even faster (he knew no one was there). I did not like that either, so I gave him the command to go out a third time. He purposely sat in front of me and gave me a look that clearly said, "Lady, don't you understand Canine? No one is there!" I realized that *I* had been the one who had broken a rule—the rule to trust your dog. I laughed, told him he was a good boy, and did not insist that he go out again. There was no body, and he knew it much better than I did; he was a free-thinking dog.

Sheep herding is another context in which a dog must be free-thinking. A dog may be given a command when working the

Photo 1.1 Scout, a free-thinking dog.

sheep but will disobey because he sees something that the handler does not see. Again, you must trust your dog. Your dog may prove to be an excellent problem solver. I remember reading about an incident in which a ewe with a newborn lamb would not move when the Border Collie working the field tried to bring her and her lamb in from the pasture. She was focused on protecting her lamb. Nothing the dog did would get the ewe to move. Instead she tried to defend her baby and attack the dog by charging at him. When she did this the lamb would follow, so the ewe stayed where she ended her charge. After a few tries, the dog repeatedly approached the ewe in such a manner that she had to keep moving toward the barn to charge after the dog. It did not take the dog long to lure the ewe and her lamb back to the barn. While this may sound like a logical solution to the problem (and it was), it was nothing the dog had done before: he had never been specifically trained to work in this manner. He'd just figured it out on his own—because he was a free-thinking dog.

Free-thinking is also an important quality in sled dogs. The lead dog of a dog sled pack is always the one to make decisions for the pack, and the one to alert the musher (the person driving the sled) about any dangers. Sometimes mushers may choose shortcut routes across frozen lakes—but if the lead dog detects that it is not safe to cross the lake, the dog will refuse to go. The smart musher trusts his dog and will not proceed. This, too, is a free-thinking dog.

Canine Intelligence

THE CASE OF CHASER, THE BORDER COLLIE

Free-thinking is not just for the workplace. Take, for example, Chaser, the Border Collie. Perhaps you've heard of her—she has, after all, become famous, featured on television, the star of countless YouTube videos, and the subject of a book. Her fame stems from her ability to identify 1022 toys by name, and to retrieve them by category. She also knows common nouns such as *house*, *ball*, and *tree*, and can even learn new words by inferential reasoning through exclusion. This means she can pick out an object—the name of which she has not been taught—by eliminating all the objects she knows. She also understands sentences with multiple elements and can learn by imitation.

Chaser is, clearly, a free-thinking dog—that is, she is a dog that has been given the training and allowed the space to make decisions of her own, and to exercise her creative potential.

People are astounded by Chaser's apparently unparalleled talent, and for good reason. Chaser is indeed exceptional in her abilities, but scientists have shown that the kind of intelligence that is foundational to her abilities is not unique to her; similar potential lies in most dogs. They have discovered that dogs understand both vocabulary and intonation of human speech using their left brain, just like people do.[1] So while Chaser is indeed a prime example of how a dog can do multiple jobs and understand multiple commands without making a mistake, she is certainly not the only example of a dog with this kind of canine intelligence (though perhaps we could say that she's the top of her class). Indeed, it is this kind of intelligence that *any* dog must have in order to be cross-trained to do different jobs.

Dogs are smarter, intellectually and emotionally, than we tend to realize, and one of the most important things a dog owner must do is to keep an opened mind about how a dog thinks, and what they know and understand. Not all dogs that are free-thinking dogs have had any special training that *make* them that way—they just *are* free-thinking, intelligent individuals. Prizes are awarded every year to dogs that have rescued people, alerted their owners to dangers, and sometimes even rescued other animals, all without special training. In fact, a recent study showed that some dogs experience empathy when they perceive that their owners are distressed and will try to rescue them.[2]

For those who are skeptical of canine intelligence, tests have been designed to try to determine how intelligent dogs are. However, there is not yet a test that can fully illustrate the intelligence of dogs—and no wonder! Unless a complex common language is developed between humans and dogs (and other animals, for that matter), we cannot completely test them.

Because we cannot give dogs an overall IQ test, scientists try to test different aspects of canine intelligence or recognition. For example, they have studied how dogs see your emotions[3] and how they process the look on your face.[4] One of the most popular ways scientists have tried to determine intelligence in dogs is by using puzzle-solving tests. (A variety of tests are available online for you to try with your dog!) And, in some recent research, scientists have determined that dogs like Chaser really do understand words that they are taught, and possibly understand them with the correct meaning.[5] In other words when a dog learns the word *walk*, he knows it means, specifically, *going for a walk* and not simply *something exciting is about to happen*. (See Chapter 3: Talking to Your Dog.) Overall, scientists are finding out that dogs are much smarter and more aware of the human world then we ever thought.

INTELLIGENCE AND BREED

There have been many books and articles written about the intelligence of dogs, some of which label certain breeds as smart and others as, well, not so smart. What the books fail to take into consideration, however, is how *biddable* (willing to obey) any given dog or breed is. This is an important oversight because we often assume that intelligence correlates with a dog's behavior, and specifically with his ability to do what he is asked, but this isn't necessarily true: you can have a dog that is not very intelligent but is very willing to do what you ask. By the same token, you can have a very intelligent dog that does not care to do what you ask.

In terms of breeds, Border Collies, Labrador Retrievers, and Golden Retrievers are often considered very smart dogs, but oftentimes what makes them test successfully is the fact that they are willing to obey, or are biddable. On the other hand, consider some of the livestock guarding breeds such as the Akbash Dog and the Anatolian Shepherd. They are bred to be independent and do not make good obedience dogs. For this reason, they often do not make the list of "intelligent" breeds. They are, however, extremely intelligent: they are bred to work on their own with vast herds of sheep and goats and often must make decisions independently about situations that they have not been specifically trained to deal with. To a lesser degree, hounds also get a bad rap. They are often difficult to train, but this is not because they are less intelligent than the working breeds. Rather, it is because they are bred to follow their nose and block out all other distractions, including you. All of these dogs are intelligent, but in their own ways. This raises the question of what, exactly, intelligence *is*: perhaps we need to rethink our concept of intelligence, for animals as well as people.

Although some dogs are bred to use their intelligence in different ways, it's important to recognize that there is also a range of intelligence in every breed. Not all dogs in a breed are the same, just like all people are not the same. The genetics of a breed, different levels of intelligence, and individual differences make it impossible to classify any breed as more or less intelligent. Therefore, when potential dog owners consider a certain breed because they have heard that this breed is "smart" or "easy to train," hopefully they will understand that intelligence and temperament can vary widely amongst individuals of any breed.

INTELLIGENCE AND TRAINING

In terms of training, dogs are capable of learning as many commands as we can dream up. They do not make mistakes by confusing one command for another, and although every dog does not demonstrate the level of skill that Chaser does, most dogs are capable of learning much more than owners teach them.

When it comes to training your dog, it is important to remember that *how* you train your dog is as important as *what* you train your dog. The reason Chaser can do what she does is because her owner taught her all of the words that she knows (the *what*) *and* taught them in a way that didn't quash or dominate her natural talents and intelligence (the *how*). Succeeding at this as a trainer or dog owner takes a lot of time and dedication.

We still have so much to learn about the mind of our dogs. It is our responsibility to give them every opportunity to use their intelligence while at the same time making sure they are safe—and safety requires a certain amount of reliable obedience.

Obedience and Free-Thinking

Training a dog successfully for SAR and other types of work, or as a pet, requires that the foundational basic training in obedience be solid but not overpowering, and that it leaves room and encourages your dog to think on his own. That being said, a free-thinking dog is not a dog that is free to disobey whenever he pleases. Whether your dog be a working dog or a pet, obedience is necessary for the safety and well-being of your dog—but obedience must not stifle or punish your dog's creativity. This balancing act between free-thinking and obedience can be cultivated with the right kind of training: training that uses positive training methods to develop a bond of trust between you and your dog.

This book and the exercises within (which include a plan and a schedule that will make it easier for your dog to learn the basic obedience lessons) are designed to help SAR, working, and pet dog handlers and owners develop a strong, foundational relationship— a relationship that is based on team work, that encourages your dog to think freely, and that will help pave the way to successful advanced and specialized training.

2

A Positive Training Philosophy

There are many reasons to give your dog basic training, and no reasons not to. A good training program will do the following:

1. Build a bond between you and your dog
2. Teach your dog how to understand the spoken word
3. Enlighten your dog as to the nature of people
4. Set rules to live by, thus eliminating confusion for your dog
5. Put order to your dog's life
6. Make your dog's existence worthwhile
7. Prevent or eliminate fear for both you and your dog
8. Build your dog's confidence
9. Keep or restore harmony in the family
10. Make dog ownership a pleasant experience
11. Help save some dogs' lives
12. Keep your dog from being re-homed

As you can see, a great deal is accomplished—and this list is far from complete—by training your dog well. It must, however, be emphasized that good training involves more than just teaching specific target behaviors to your dog; it also involves the method you use to teach your dog.

Just like you, your dog will be exposed to many novel situations and environments throughout his life to which he will have to react and respond. Basic training is the foundation upon which his responses will be based: it is the bedrock for everything that is to come. Basic training involves first teaching skills and commands, then using what has been learned in novel situations, but it is important to remember that successful basic training requires more than understanding the individual *steps* for basic obedience; think of it instead as a complete system and an ongoing process. Once your dog learns the basic commands, he needs to practice them in a variety of life situations, and then apply them to the unplanned, real-life situations he will be in every day. This is a life-long project.

The Training Philosophy

Some people may think that having a training philosophy does not matter—that you simply train your dog. This couldn't be further from the truth. Before you start working with your dog, it is a good idea to sort out exactly what you believe about your dog, and about dogs in general. What you believe about your dog will communicate itself through the way you talk, move, and handle your dog during training—and your dog will understand.

Dogs are very intelligent. They understand much more than the average dog owner gives them credit for. But when people talk about training their dog, they tend to use phrases like: "I have to teach my dog *how* to sit." In my experience, this is the wrong attitude for a dog owner to have: it neglects the fact that your dog already knows how to do everything that you want to teach him. He is born knowing how to sit, walk, lie down, get on and off of things—in

> Obedience training is not teaching your dog *how* to do anything. He already knows how to do it! Rather, you will be teaching him signals that tells him what to do.

short, he already knows how to move his body. What you must understand and practice, then, is that you are not teaching your dog *how* to do anything. You are only teaching your dog the words you will use to signal him to perform a specific action.

People who think that they must teach a dog how to do something often feel that they must bully the dog to get him to do it. I see this as a subconscious reaction to the word *how*. Once you accept the fact that you do not have to teach a dog how to do anything and that your task is instead to build a bridge of communication with the dog, the task of training will be a much smoother and happier one for both you and your dog. By accepting this concept, your dog will enjoy training and you will build a wonderful, trusting relationship together. This relationship, this bond, can run very deep.

It is hard for some dog owners to remember that their dogs are not human and do not interpret the world as we do. It is, therefore, worth emphasizing how important it is to remember that dogs, because of the unique ways in which their senses take in information, do not view the world from a human point of view, but from their own. What is important to your dog is not necessarily important to you. Think, for example, of a dog's need to sniff everything, even things we humans find unpleasant. The world of scent is as important to a dog as sight is to humans. Their noses and ears being their keenest sense organs, dogs explore their world primarily through smells and sounds.

From a dog's point of view, many of the things we ask them to do make no canine sense at all. For example, a dog that is walking by himself in your yard does not sit every time he stops, yet this is what we ask our dogs to do in the *heel* exercise. A dog will sit in a *heel* exercise because he wants to please us, or because we have made it worthwhile for him to do it. By making it worthwhile, you are motivating your dog to do what you ask him to do.

When I'm training, I like to motivate my dogs with a combination of a clicker, treats, and a good old pat on the head. But every dog has different motivators, so each method will work best in different circumstances, and these circumstances will be different for every dog. This is because dog personalities are as varied as those of people. While it is true that some breeds tend to have one type of personality or inherited trait (such as a desire to find birds or herd sheep), you will find a huge range in personalities even within breeds: what works with one dog of a particular breed may not work as well with another of the same breed.

You will need to take the time to find what motivates your dog as an individual. To do this, you will probably need to try different things; toys, treats, and games are a good place to start. (Although it is rare, a true working dog is motived by the work that he does. I was fortunate to own such a dog.) While I have found that clicker training works with 99 percent of dogs, it is important not to take any training advice as dogma, but as suggestions: pay attention to what your dog responds to and to what motivates him. By understanding the individual mind and nature of your dog, you can better develop your own, personal philosophy that works toward a deep bond, happy relationship, and successful training.

Positive Versus Negative Training Methods

There are many trainers and training books out there, making it difficult to determine which ones are good and which ones to avoid. As a general rule, any trainer that uses outdated methods or any book written by someone who is not recognized by a respectable organization should be avoided. Further, understanding a little about the different methods of training will help you determine what is good and what is not. In this section I will help you understand the basics of some of the different methods of training.

Some of the methods that were and continue to be used were written prior, during, and right after World War II, and are based on the way military and police dogs were and are often trained. These methods employ choke chains, prong collars, and, in more recent times, shock collars, and involve harsh treatment of the dogs, using pain and punishment to correct and "teach" dogs. These "jerk-and-hurt" methods were the only popular methods when I started training dogs in the early 1960s, and I have witnessed their results. It didn't take long for me to observe that, although dogs trained using this method could execute behaviors with competition-level precision, many times they were clearly unhappy and were not having fun.

So, as early the late 1960s and early 1970s, I started experimenting with kinder dog training methods. Today, these are referred to as *positive training methods*, and they are the basis of the methods used in this book. Positive dog training methods are a complex system of training that uses positive reinforcement, instead of punishment, as its basis. Trainers that use positive methods are very selective about negative reinforcements, which may, in some cases, still be appropriate. Any negative reinforcement necessary often involves withdrawing the reward rather than physically hurting the dog.

> Positive training methods build a positive bond between you and your dog and create a dog that is happy to work with you.

Some people may think that positive training methods were discovered fairly recently, but this is not the case. The success of positive training methods was recognized as early as World War I, when the head trainer for the British war dog program, Major Colonel Richardson,[1] emphatically stated in his books that positive training methods were the only methods that produced reliable war dogs. However, training methods went downhill by World War II, a time when many misconceptions about dogs were proliferated by both scientists and dog trainers. While we have since learned better, there are still trainers worldwide, as well as prominent figures in dog-related media, who employ these harmful methods.

Everything works *some* of the time and *nothing* works *all* of the time! But that does not mean you should employ harsh training methods.

Some people swear by those methods—and indeed, it should be noted that these methods *can* work with some dogs—but just because a method that employs pain and fear may work in some circumstances for some dogs does not mean that you should use it. As with motivating your dog, it is important to keep in mind that

It is especially damaging to use jerk-and-hurt methods with puppies and small dogs, even if the method is mildly employed. Young and small dogs are especially susceptible to physical and mental trauma.

everything works *some* of the time and *nothing* works *all* of the time. This is a concept that is not usually mentioned by advocates of these types of methods, who skip over the fact that, while some dogs are trainable under these circumstances, many are not. Many dogs cannot handle this type of training, and thus fail these training programs.

More than this, many of the old methods do not foster a positive relationship with your dog. In some cases, a dog will learn to fear people, especially you, and even though some dogs will obey using the harsh methods, they will not do it willingly or happily. They will do it because they are traumatized.

It is important to understand that dogs and humans share almost all of the same feelings and emotions such as joy, sadness, anticipation, and fear. Dogs, like people, will learn quickly when they are focused on avoiding further trauma, but this learning comes with a lot of pain. Recall an incident in which you or someone you know was severely frightened. Most people, like dogs, never forget such a traumatic event. It is not a good memory and often comes with negative associations. We don't want this for ourselves, and I believe that no dog-loving owner wants this for his dog.

Obedience as Self-Control

It is hard to remember that learning something, thoroughly knowing it, and applying it are three different steps. Often dog owners expect their dogs to be robots that flawlessly perform every time they are told. This sets the dog owner and dog up for failure.

Once your dog has learned his exercises or his jobs, no matter what they are, he will be able to do them for long sessions as needed and will not forget his lessons over time. But learning is exhausting. For this reason, teaching takes patience. (Again, think of how different it was for you between learning something new and doing what you know and like.) Even when your dog has learned a command, it may be the case that he does not perform it consistently. Dog owners often become upset when they feel that their dog knows a command but refuses to do it. It is, however, very important to understand that once a dog has been trained to follow a command, *obedience is not a question of knowing what to do, but the ability to exercise the self-control to do it*. This is as true for people as it is for dogs.

Dogs do not disobey out of vengeance or to be nasty; rather, they do what seems best to them, based on what they feel is right. This is driven by their needs, instincts, and desires. It takes time and practice

> Obedience is not a question of knowing *what* to do, but the dog's ability to exercise *self-control* to do it. Building self-control takes time and practice.

for a dog to do what *you* want rather than what *he* wants—and in some cases, a dog may disobey a command because he really does know best. Take SAR dogs, for example. If the SAR dog signals that there is something in an area that needs investigation, and the handler tries to call the dog to leave the area without investigating it (a problem that many new SAR dog handlers encounter, often due to a lack of trust in the handler/dog working relationship), the dog *should disobey* the call to leave. Rather than following his handler, he should insist that the handler stay and investigate what he has found. Guide dogs for the blind are another good example. These dogs may disobey when their handler tells them to go forward but they know there is danger in doing so. The dog will not go forward but will instead lead the person around the danger or away from it and in some cases not move at all. This is called *intelligent disobedience* and is a trained response for certain circumstances.

Above all, when it comes to obedience training, the key word is *patience*. Training dogs takes time and practice. By understanding dogs and not expecting more from them than we do from ourselves, we will have fairer relationships with the dogs we work with. After all, they are feeling, thinking beings, just like us.

Now that we're clear on the goals of positive training methods and the importance of fostering free thinking in your dog, it's time to start setting up to train your dog by going over a few pre-training basics. The chapters in Part II will cover topics including communication, choosing a trainer, selecting food and treats, housetraining and crate training, and grooming your dog.

Part II

Pre-Training Basics for the Free-Thinking Dog Trainer

3

Talking to Your Dog

Many dog owners do not think about how they talk to their dogs. This is because talking is very basic to humans. We change our pitch and tonalization, and we add facial expressions without thinking about them. Often, we do this as a reaction to our emotions, situation, and expectations. For the most part, we are good at these kinds of communication—at least when we are talking to another human. But what does all that talk mean to our dogs? This chapter will help you understand the communication gaps that may exist between you and your dog, and help you begin to bridge them. The exercises that follow in Part III are designed to further instill clear communication between you and your dog.

Speech Is a Foreign Language to a Dog

To the best of our knowledge, dogs to not have a spoken language like ours. Although dogs do not use language the way humans do, they do have a complex system of communication that is composed of the tone and volume of their vocalizations, their body language, and their spatial relationship to other animals and people.

A dog's body language not only involves his vocalizations and spatial relationships, but also includes his facial expressions, the position and movement of his tail and ears, the position of the hair on his back and neck, and the degree of stiffness in his movements.

Dogs can also read the body language of other animals: for example, dogs have no difficulty reading a cat's body language and understanding whether the cat is friendly or hostile. In fact, dogs are also excellent at reading *us*, and they learn quickly even though our body language is not exactly like theirs. Studies have shown that dogs can read how you feel by the look on your face, and understand the emotions that go along with that look.[1,2] They will read and react to your facial expression and emotions before they will react to what you say.

This is no surprise—many dogs, ever since they were puppies, have had nothing to do all day but study people, and they get very good at it. It's good to remember that you can learn to read what your dog is feeling, too: although we don't speak the same language, some forms of communication are universal! With some practice and study of canine body language,[3] you will be able to better understand both how your dog communicates what he is feeling though his body language, and how you are communicate to your dog with your own body language.

You should be aware, however, that dogs—especially puppies that have not had a lot of experience with people—are also capable of misunderstanding your body language. (As an aside, the fact that dogs can misunderstand and misread our body language is another great reason to study canine body language. Being able to tell when your dog has and has not properly understood you can be very useful for training.) Dogs can misunderstand because, until they learn from experience what people are all about, a dog is going to interpret you in terms of dog language.

The takeaway is this: how you move, how you sound, and how you look—your body language as well as your facial expressions—are very important to a dog. People are generally surprised at how much their attitude comes through in their tone of voice and their body language. The person who is not sure that his dog is going to respond to his command may sound doubtful or questioning. The dog will pick up on this right away and respond accordingly.

It is rather amazing how adept dogs are at communicating with us even though we do not have a common spoken language. Just think of how your dog lets you know what he wants—like wanting to go out to do his business—by mostly using body language such as gestures, looks, and movements.

But what about verbal communication? Given that dogs do not use human language to communicate, the question becomes how to communicate with your dog using verbal commands. In reality, dogs do not understand words *that they are not taught*. They will not automatically know where one word ends and another begins. For this reason, you should never repeat a command to your dog. He will not understand that when you say, "Sit-sit-sit," you are telling him three times to sit. He will learn, instead, that *sit-sit-sit* is one word or sound, and he may learn never to sit until the third *sit* leaves your lips. This can be a frustrating outcome, but your dog is, in fact, likely doing exactly what you showed him to do: most people, after two failed attempts, will physically encourage their dog to sit on the third command. Therefore, when you give a command to your dog, it should be immediately followed by a response—either your dog should sit, or you should enforce the command.

A NOTE ON THE USE OF DIFFERENT COMMANDS

You will notice that I recommend using different commands for similar behaviors. This is because each one has its own purpose. It is necessary that every exercise, and every variation on an exercise, be associated with a different, unique command. If you do not have a different command or word, your dog will not understand that a new rule is in play or that a specific and different behavior (even if subtly different from another) is expected of him. This miscommunication between you and your dog can cause confusion and your dog may not do what you want. Miscommunication and confusion set your dog up for failure and set you up for frustration. Keep in mind that, just like people, dogs like instructions that are made clear for them.

By using different commands, I have successfully trained several of my SAR dogs to perform various, distinct SAR disciplines and other jobs, and they have never made a mistake. For example, each dog can perform air-scenting work (looking for human scent in general); scent-specific work (looking for an identified scent); cadaver detection (looking for cadaver scent above ground, in ground, and in the water); and disaster work. Some of my SAR dogs have also worked as toxic mold–detection dogs and as livestock herding dogs.

Training a dog for different SAR disciplines is not easy. It requires daily or weekly training and years-long commitment to not only complete initial training in each discipline, but also to keep that training up-to-date. In reality, then, this type of training is complete when the dog retires. This is an intense process, and it is important to keep in mind that not every person or dog will succeed at cross-training.

TONE OF VOICE MATTERS

You will have more success working with your dog if you maintain an attitude that expects them to respond correctly. The tone of your voice when you talk to your dog should be one of authority. Many people "ask" their dog a command, using an almost pleading tone of

Speak to your dog with a tone of voice that says you expect the dog to obey. Give the command (e.g., "Sit") only one time, and ensure that there is an immediate response: either your dog should sit, or you should enforce the command.

voice or raising their tone slightly at the end of the word. Even to a person, this would sound like a question—and it feels that way to a dog, too. So, to the dog, the owner is saying, "Sit, please sit. Do you feel like sitting?" Often, owners also give body signals that reinforce this tone of voice. Because the owners who have this mindset typically do not enforce the command, the dog learns that when he is addressed with this tone of voice he does not have to obey. The tone you use with your dog should be a statement of fact with an attitude that communicates that you expect him to obey.

Speaking with authority does not, however, mean speaking very loudly or talking to your dog in an unpleasant, mean, or angry way. Enforcing a command does not mean bullying or getting physically harsh. Many people will raise their voice when they become frustrated, or when they think that the dog did not hear them. In fact, it is very unlikely (unless he is deaf) that your dog didn't hear you. As we know, dogs have very sensitive hearing. If your dog is near you—say, by your side—he can hear your stomach gurgling if you are hungry. He can even hear you breathing. A dog that appears as though he can't hear you is, in reality, probably just ignoring you. Because of this, simply raising your voice is unlikely to solve the problem. And remember, if you consistently raise your voice when you are training your dog, he may learn not to respond *unless* you raise your voice. This could be embarrassing in public. It is best for both you and your dog that you teach your dog to respond to the normal level of your voice, and even to a whisper if he is close.

SHOW YOUR DOG WHAT YOU WANT: NON-VERBAL SIGNALS AND COMMUNICATION

As I mentioned earlier, people forget that their dogs do not understand our language the same way we do. What makes this even more difficult to remember is that our dogs *do* learn the meaning of certain words. However, at the level of the sentence, it is unclear how much they actually understand.[4]

For this reason, it is important to *show* a dog what you want rather than trying to *tell* him what you want. If you think of communicating with your dog as you would

Show a dog what you want: do not try to tell him. Dogs do not speak our language, but they understand body language.

with a person who does not speak your language and comes from a different culture, you will be on the right track!

Because dogs are so attuned to body language, non-verbal signals can be very successfully used in training. Some of the obedience exercises in this book employ a hand signal to help show your dog what you want him to do. In many cases, the dog will eventually learn to respond to the hand signal even when it is not accompanied by a verbal command. Many trick dog trainers (including myself) use subtle hand signals, facial expressions, and body movements to signal a dog to do a specific trick. Since a dog's means of communication involves body language, they naturally respond to non-verbal signals.

One mistake people often make, especially with puppies, is to try to give the puppy a command while they are smiling or laughing at the puppy's silly antics. As scientists have discovered, dogs laugh themselves, so they understand laughter.[5] The puppy, therefore, quickly learns that you are not serious, and may even understand laughter as a reward for his behavior, encouraging him to act sillier in order to get you to laugh more.

While you do not have to act angry when working with your dog, you will be more successful if you act, look, and sound serious. For adult dogs, your tone of voice during training sessions should be no-nonsense. (It can be happier with puppies, though you should maintain focus on training and avoid being distracted by the puppy's attempt to play.)

In my experience, having a confident, no-nonsense attitude is essential to communicating effectively with your dog during basic training. For one thing, having the right attitude can help you control the chemical signals you send to your dog. When your emotions change, your body chemistry changes in a variety of ways, and dogs are able to detect these changes by scent. This is why you've probably heard that dogs "smell" fear—in fact, they are smelling the chemical changes that occur in your body as part of your fear response. Beyond helping you have the right smell, the right attitude can also help you to use effective body language and tone of voice to successfully train your dog.

Without realizing it, your attitude is communicated through your body language and tone of voice, which, as we have seen, are important routes of communication for dogs. During a training session,

> Once you know your dog is reliable, your tone of voice can relax a bit. This is when the partnership with your dog can really deepen.

then, your attitude should communicate that when you give a command, there is no question about whether or not your dog is going to respond. You must sound as if there is no doubt in your mind that they are going to respond properly. Your confidence in your dog's ability to respond will give your dog confidence as well.

Although I speak of having a stern, no-nonsense attitude when giving your dog a command, it is important to understand that this is only necessary until your dog understands what he is and is not to do in the context of basic training. As the dog learns to work with you and has learned what you want to teach him, the attitude should be one of a team working together. You are the leader, but otherwise you and your dog are equal. I have found this to be the most beautiful relationship with a working dog: the time when you both trust each other.

WHEN YOUR DOG DOESN'T LISTEN

There are six common reasons why a dog will not respond to a command:

1. The dog was not taught the command well enough for him to understand it.

2. The dog has learned that the owner will not enforce the command either at all or until repeating the command.

3. The dog is not paying attention because he has not yet developed the required self-control.

4. The owner's body language communicates a different message than the spoken command.

5. The owner has not motivated the dog in a positive manner to obey.

6. The owner talks to his dog too much during training and/ or work.

While it is okay to talk to your dog when you are not training or working, you should not have conversations with your dog while training or working. This is one of the biggest mistakes that SAR dog handlers and pet owners make. Talking too much can distract your dog from the job at hand or confuse him. Remember that many of your words are only noise to your dog.

Thinking about how you sound, look, and move, and even practicing using the right tone of voice before you train your dog, will go a long way to bridging the communication gap that exists between you and your dog.

Do Not Scold Your Dog

So, you come home to discover that your dog went through the trash while you were out. He had a good time being a scavenger, and he was rewarded by his scavenging behavior because of the good things he found and ate in the trash. Now, hours later, you see the trash scattered about the house, get very upset, and start yelling at your dog. You might grab him, show him the trash, and put him in his crate as punishment.

Sound familiar? It is common to scold when a person (often a child) disobeys a command. Scolding can be an effective strategy with other humans who speak the same language—but does it accomplish anything with a dog? This section will show you how your dog may interpret scolding.

Many people will scold their dog when he makes a mistake because they feel that the dog is intentionally disobeying them. This is not only a misinterpretation of your dog's behavior (it is more likely that the dog has not developed the self-control to obey you), but also a misunderstanding of what scolding will actually communicate to your dog. Take the trash example above: after a few repetitions of this scenario, the dog will learn that every time there is trash on the floor and the owner comes through the door after being gone for a while, the owner is not nice to be near. Despite knowing this, the dog is still happy to see the owner. But instead of running up to the owner the way he normally does, he slinks or behaves in an unsure manner. The owner assumes that the dog knows he did something wrong (getting into the trash) because the dog looks "guilty." In reality, however, the dog is nervous about how the owner will behave. Never in a million years will the dog make the connection that it was his behavior (going into the trash hours before), rather than just the fact of trash on the floor, that has caused the owner's anger.

Scolding does not teach the dog what to do, nor does it point out what he did wrong. Think about it: the dog will only learn that your behavior is erratic since you go from being nice to being nasty. And because you are being nasty, and the dog can feel and see that you are angry or upset, it will also teach him that he does not want to be near you when you are scolding. Your dog does not understand your words or explanations while you are scolding; he only knows what he sees, smells, and hears: your body language, chemical signals, and tone of voice. As a rule of thumb, if you get to the point where you feel angry or have the urge to scold, stop training.

Above all, it is very important to your dog's safety that you never scold or otherwise reprimand your dog if he comes to you after he has done something that you do not like. Imagine your dog running into oncoming traffic. Like most people, you would yell harshly, with fear in your voice, for your dog to come. If your dog does not trust you and has learned to stay away from you when you sound unpleasant, he will most likely run away from you rather than come towards you and away from the danger. It is imperative for your dog's well-being that he learn to trust you and to come when called, no matter how you sound.

So remember: scolding never teaches your dog what you intend to teach him, and the fact that scolding may make you feel better by letting you vent is not an excuse. After all, your dog does not understand the words you are using to scold him, and he does not interpret the context of your behavior in the same way you do.

Taking the time to develop solid, clear communication between you and your dog is essential to developing a good relationship and successfully training your dog. The next chapter will look into some key questions to consider before you move on to training your dog.

4

Questions to Ask Before You Start Training

The information in this chapter is meant to address three important questions: who should train the dog, when should training begin, and what should the dog be fed? While these are not necessarily the first questions that come to the mind of the new dog trainer, they are questions that must be asked, and answered, before you begin.

Who Should Train the Dog?

HAVING ONE TRAINER

Whether you are training a working dog or a family pet, it is always best to have only one trainer. When I tell my clients this, especially if they are training a pet, the first thing I tend to hear is, "But I want my dog to listen to everyone in the family!" The desire to have a dog that listens beautifully to all members of the family, and maybe even to guests, leads many people to think that they must get the whole family to work with the dog from the beginning of a dog's training program. But this could not be further from the truth.

After your dog is trained, mature, and experienced, it may come to pass that your dog is able to work well with and listen to many individuals. Indeed, if the training is done well, your dog *will* listen to everyone you want him to once he has learned all of his commands, but instituting a multitrainer method from the get-go is not the best way to have your dog learn his commands efficiently and reliably. In fact, it can hinder much more than it helps. This is because every person handles a dog differently, and to a dog, these differences—which include voice, attitude, vocabulary, and body language, among others—amount, in the beginning, to different dialects. To give the more straightforward example, it is not uncommon for different people in the family to use different commands. One family member may use the word *drop* to mean *down,* while another will just use *down.* Using more than one command for the same behavior will confuse the dog as to what he is supposed to do. Moreover, the timing of the steps in each exercise is critical in the beginning of training and each person will not have the same timing. And of course, different individuals will use different body movements to execute the same commands. Again, movement is a very important form of communication for the dog and bombarding the dog with many different movements that are meant to communicate the same thing will confuse the dog.

It is not fair to the dog to ask him to learn his commands in many different dialects at the same time. It would be like giving him a constant multilingual vocabulary test, and the confusion that results from this kind of training may lead the dog to not respond at all, which can cause frustration for the person trying to train the dog. In some cases, intense the confusion may even lead to untraining what the dog has already learned.

CHOOSING THE TRAINER

When there can only be one trainer, the next question is, of course, Who should it be? People sometimes are not sure how to make this decision. In the end, this is a personal choice and can depend on the dog's relationship with each person, but there are a few guidelines to keep in mind.

If you are laying the groundwork for the dog to have a job, the choice is simple: the trainer should be the person who is going to handle and work with the dog on the job.

In other contexts, the first choice of trainer should be the person who is best able to physically handle the dog. Consider the size and strength of the dog and the person who is going to train the dog. Initially, the dog may pull. The trainer must be strong enough

> In the context of family pets, one adult in the family must be the person to train the dog. In the context of working dogs, the person who is going to handle the dog should be the person to train the dog.

to hold the dog without using harsh methods and equipment. For this reason, and even though many parents feel that they want their children to be involved early, it is best that the trainer be an adult. To make the point clear, imagine a 10-year-old child trying to handle a St. Bernard or Great Dane. This could be a dangerous combination and may put the safety of the child and the dog at risk. It should also be noted that some of the issues that come up in training may be too complex for a child to handle.

The next important factor in choosing a trainer is to consider who has the time to spend working with the dog. While the minimum training session per day can be as little as 15 minutes, more is always better.

A third factor to consider in some cases is who the dog responds to best. Some people feel that the dog should be handled by the person that the dog ignores the most so that the dog will learn to listen to that person. In my experience, this is often not a good idea because a dog might have some very good reasons for ignoring someone. For instance, a dog may ignore someone because he senses that that person does not feel confident around him. Alternatively, the dog may have attached himself to one person in particular; these dogs are called "one-man dogs." While this phenomenon occurs in varying degrees, certain breeds are bred to be more attached to one person. The dog feels right doing this. It does not mean that they do not like the other family members, just that they prefer one particular person. This is no different than you or me hitting it off more with one person than another.

Remember that training is a learning process for the dog. Just as you had favorite teachers in school from whom you enjoyed learning, and others with whom you didn't connect, so will the dog. If the dog has more respect for one person and responds better to him or her, that is the person who should train the dog.

After the training program is completed and the dog has learned his exercises, everyone in the family can practice with the dog so long as they, too, understand the exercises and commands. Since the dog will be easier to handle once trained, it will be easier at this point for anyone who originally had difficulty handling the dog to work with him. After the lessons are completed and the dog is obedient, the youngsters in the family can work with the dog under adult supervision.

When Should I Train My Dog?

TRAINING THE PUPPY

While you can train a dog of any age, if you have a puppy or plan to get one, keep in mind that puppyhood (between eight weeks and three months of age) is an excellent time to lay the foundation for good behavior and obedience training. The old rule that you must wait until a dog is six months old to start training is incorrect. Your puppy is learning all the time, whether you train him or not.

It is better that you teach the puppy what you want him to learn rather than letting him form his own rules. That being said, most puppies do have to mature before they can learn to apply their lessons and develop self-control. Training may begin, but does not end, with puppyhood.

Training a puppy can be fun as well as challenging. All puppies can learn their basic obedience exercises, but unlike older dogs, a puppy may seem to know the exercise today and then forget it tomorrow. In reality, your puppy has not completely forgotten what you taught him; he simply needs some time to put it all together and be able to perform what he knows consistently. Because of this, you have to keep working regularly with the puppy, often reteaching him until he gets it.

Dogs that will have jobs or enter competitions, however, will require more advanced and specialized training as they get older. It is worth noting that the training methods you use with a puppy will differ from those used for formal training with older dogs—but solid puppy training will lay the groundwork for this more formal training later on, which will include specific exercises that are required for the sport or job that the dog will be doing.

> Just like small children, the world is completely new to a puppy. Everything is exciting and must be explored. The puppy has very little life experience to which he can relate his lessons and experiences, and learning will take time. Training must be done gently, slowly, and with lots of patience.

Puppyhood can, for example, be the best time to teach the *sit* and *recall* (or *come*) exercises—and teaching them is easy to do. Puppies generally want to come to you and are very willing to do what you ask, if you ask correctly.

Every time you want your puppy to come to you, use his name and then say, "Come," in a very happy, inviting tone. When the puppy comes to you, give him a treat and make a big fuss over him. Practice this in a safe environment, either indoors or in a fenced-in outdoor area.

You can also call the puppy at feeding time and say, "Come," just before he reaches you to be fed. It

> Never trust a puppy off-leash in an area where he can run away. This is especially true of the hounds and hunting breeds, for whom the instinct to follow scent is stronger than the instinct to listen to you.

is important that the puppy learns that coming to you is always fun! When the puppy comes to you, after he gets his treat or food for coming, you can use another treat held over his head (as explained in the *sit* exercise, discussed in Chapter 9) to teach him to sit when he comes to you.

Beyond the basic foundations of obedience training, puppyhood is a great time to get your dog used to being handled (see Chapter 6: Handling Your Dog's Body for Grooming and Hygiene). It is also the most important time to socialize your dog, something that must be done with all dogs. This can be done by arranging playdates with other puppies that you know or through puppy kindergarten classes. Keep in mind that socialization must be gradual so as to not frighten or overwhelm your puppy.

TAKING BREAKS: AVOIDING ANGER AND FRUSTRATION

Training any dog takes patience, but we all have bad days when our patience and tolerance level drops significantly. Often this state of mind has nothing to do with our dogs. If you are having a day when you cannot be happy, upbeat, and patient with your dog, it is best not to train your dog. When you are upset, you cannot explain to your dog, as you could to a friend or family member, that he

> If you or your dog are having a bad day, take a break from training. Skipping a day or two will not cause either of you to lose what you have gained.

is not the object of your bad mood. This could cause all sorts of negative feelings for your dog. If either of you feels frustration or anger, learning will stop and resentment or avoidance of training may start.

It is also important to remember that even on good days, everybody will have a different level of patience. Know your level and your limits, because training your dog can really be a test of patience. Some dogs—especially puppies, but dogs of any age—may seem to understand what you want today, and tomorrow act as though they've never learned anything at all, leaving you feeling like you're getting nowhere. This is frustrating! Patience is something we all have to work on, but if you find you consistently have a lot of trouble being patient with your dog, you might consider having someone else do the training. It is better to recognize your limits than to put your relationship with your dog in jeopardy.

Remember, also, that you may not be the only one getting frustrated. Think of a time in your life when you had to learn something new, such as at new job or in school: you were probably exhausted by the end of the lesson or training. Your dog can feel the same way. Learning is very difficult and tiring for both animals and people. Your dog will have his own limits during a session, after which he will not be able to take any more training. What's more, dogs, like you and me, can have bad days, too. They may not feel well on a given day but are not actually sick. Dogs try to communicate this to us, but the communication is often very subtle: they may simply not work well that day, move a bit slower, or not pay attention as much as they normally do.

> If your dog suddenly brings less energy and enthusiasm to training than usual, he might just be having a bad day. Be sure to observe your dog over the next several days; if the behavior persists for more than a few days, he may actually be sick.

In the case of dog training, less can sometimes mean more. Following the *5-1-5-1-5-quit Training Formula* outlined in Chapter 8 will help you keep training sessions to a manageable length. As well, never be afraid to take a break. In some cases, taking a break is simply what is best. You will not backslide if you skip training for a half or even a whole day. There have been times when I have even instructed clients to stop training their dogs for an entire week. Both the clients and the dogs were much more successful in their training after doing so.

What Should I Feed My Dog?

TREATS AND TRAINING

Training, both the traditional way and using a clicker, entails the use of treats. This section will guide you on how to properly use treats.

I am surprised at how many people still believe that it is wrong to use treats to train their dog. These people tend to think that if they use treats, the dog will learn to *only* work for treats. This is simply not true.

Conversely, other people are convinced that their dog is not food-motivated and that treats won't work at all. In these cases, I say you simply have not found the right treat.

There are, of course, exceptional cases. Some dogs are so motivated by food that it is all they will focus on. In these cases, treats can still be used in initial training, but you should wean the dog off treats as soon as possible. In the case of a dog that is especially unmotivated by food, using a treat won't hurt training; he will learn what you want regardless, and may sometimes still be happy for the tasty reward. In general, though, dogs tend to learn quicker with a treat rather than without one.

The secret to using treats in training is to be sure that the treats are

- something the dog really loves;
- only given to the dog during training; and
- very small.

The treat should be a tease, not a meal. It is okay to train before a meal so that the dog is hungry and will want the treat more, but treats should not replace regular food. This being the case, you should keep in mind that in the beginning of training you may be treating your dog quite a bit. Especially if the dog is small, be sure to adjust his food intake to compensate for the extra calories. We do not want your dog to get fat.

While dogs do not have the same number of taste buds as people do, they can tell the difference between sweet, salty, and bitter. They rely on their sense of smell to determine the "taste" of a treat. The treat you use with your dog should be something he loves. In human terms, a treat is the same as a favorite snack, like potato chips or nuts. You will have to experiment with different treats to see what your dog can't get enough of, and keep in mind that treats can sometimes be found in unexpected places. "People food" may do the trick, and, in my experience, few dogs can resist dry cat food.

The treat should also be small—about ¼-inch in size. You must be able to hold a few treats in the palm of your hand and dispense them easily, which means that mushy or soft things such as soft cheese will not work. Fruit and vegetables, on the other hand, can work well. I've certainly known some dogs that just love raw carrots!

A few easy treats that I have found are

> Treats used to train a dog should be around ¼-inch in size. They should be things the dog loves and only gets during training. "People food" is okay for treats!

- small bacon bits such as you buy for salads;
- Charlee Bear treats, which are made for training and only have about three calories per treat;
- thinly sliced hot dogs that have been nuked crispy in a microwave (though not so crispy that they are brittle and difficult to handle); and
- thinly sliced, pre-cooked breakfast sausage.

Once you find the treats your dog loves, make sure that he only gets them when he is in training. They must be a special prize for doing what you ask him to do.

CHOOSING THE RIGHT FOOD

Your dog must be on a high-quality dog food. There are many debates about what is and is not high quality (I could write an entire book about the subject), but one thing is for sure: nothing you can buy at the grocery store or discount store, and half of what is available in pet shops, is not the quality you want. There are a number of good websites that evaluate the quality of both dog food and treats, and these can be excellent resources for selecting a high-quality food for your dog. *The Dog Food Advisor: Saving Good Dogs from Bad Food*[1] and chewy.com are both good places to buy food and treats. You may pay more for the better dog food and treats, but in most cases you will be getting more bang for your buck: your dog will not have to eat as much to get the nutrition he needs, making the cost per serving less than that of lower quality food. And of course, there is the priceless, long-term benefit of your dog being healthier and living longer.

High-quality food not only makes your dog healthier, but can also have an effect on the dog's behavior and performance. Consider how much better a person feels on a wholesome diet as opposed to a diet of junk food. The same is true for your dog. A young dog may look healthy on poor food, but later in life (and sometimes as early as one year old) he will pay for it, and so will you with veterinary visits.

It is also okay for dogs to eat "people food." In some cases there is nothing healthier for them. We are not talking about junk food, but rather table scraps such as meat, potatoes, and cooked vegetables, as well as raw fruit and vegetables that are added to his regular food. In fact, recent research has shown that feeding certain vegetables can help reduce the chance of cancer in dogs.

By contrast, many of the lesser-quality dog foods contain cancer-causing chemicals and ingredients.[2] Be aware, however, that there are certain fruits and vegetables that are not good for dogs, including onions, raisins, and grapes.

Another misconception people have about dog food, which companies use to sell products, is the claim that dogs should eat what they would normally eat "in the wild," as if they were wolves—that is, they should eat meat, and lots of it. Of course in reality, wolves, like all wild animals, are only able to eat what they can find. Wolves are scavengers, and scavenging does not necessarily mean a healthy diet. In the end, what is most important to remember (what dog food companies fail to mention) is that dogs are not wolves, and they have different dietary needs.

Some who believe "in the wild" diet believe in feeding their dogs raw meat, but this can be very dangerous for a dog. All of my veterinarians over the years have told me not to feed raw meat to dogs because of the risk of bacterial infection. (And anyway, who knows? If a dog could cook meat on his own, he might prefer that to eating raw!)

It is also important to recognize that dogs are omnivores, not carnivores: they are scavengers and will eat anything that they can find, meat or otherwise. They can also digest things, such as grain, that wolves cannot.[3] In fact, it seems that dogs *should* have grain in their diets. Recently, the American Food and Drug Administration (FDA) announced that dogs that are on grain-free diets have a greater risk of developing canine dilated cardiomyopathy (DCM).[4] The only time a dog owner should avoid a certain type grain for their dog is if the dog is allergic to that specific grain.

The questions answered in this chapter aren't necessarily the first that might come to mind when beginning to train your dog, but they're all important to consider before you begin, and will help prepare you and your dog for positive, successful training sessions, a better relationship, and overall good mental and physical health. The next chapter will look at a couple of important bits of training to do with your dog before beginning formal obedience training: housetraining and crate training.

5

Housetraining and Crate Training

Both housetraining and crate training are best done while the dog is a puppy. That being said, it is not impossible to teach adult dogs as well. The older dog will need more time and patience, but all dogs like to have a space of their own that is clean.

Housetraining

Dogs are often surrendered for adoption because the owner was unsuccessful in housetraining the dog when it was a puppy. Housetraining is the responsibility of the dog's owner, and by understanding how to housetrain a dog or puppy, you have a much higher chance of success.

The difficulty or ease with which a puppy or dog is housetrained depends on the age of the dog, the conditions in which the dog was raised, and its breed. Of course, it is best to housetrain a dog as a puppy, but in some cases you may have an older dog that needs to be housetrained. If the dog has been raised in a kennel or outdoor environment, he has likely been able to relieve himself whenever he feels the need. It can be difficult for such a dog to transition to an indoor household situation in which he must learn to wait. Even when you adopt a dog that has already been housetrained, there is always the question of schedule and timing.

In some cases, a dog that has been adopted is used to a different schedule and will need help adjusting to your schedule.

Keep in mind that some puppies that have been raised in unhygienic environments (i.e., those in which they had to live in and near their toilet area) were denied their natural desire to keep their living area clean and may have been subject to other abuses. Because of lack of food, some dogs may have even learned to eat their own or other dogs' feces. It will take keen observation to determine if your dog or puppy is successfully housetrained, or whether he is actually just cleaning up his own mess. Housetraining these dogs will require diligence, compassion, and understanding.

Some housetraining problems cannot be solved by training. It is not uncommon for a grown female dog to be unable to hold a full bladder, which may be the result of a weak sphincter or due to being spayed. In other cases, the dog or puppy may have a urinary tract infection. In these cases, dogs will go frequently, may show discomfort, and will not produce a lot of urine each time they go. If you suspect any medical issues, or even if you are not sure, take your dog for a veterinarian check-up. It is not fair to try to housetrain a dog that cannot help himself.

Breed also plays a role in housetraining. In general, the smaller the dog the more difficult it may be to housetrain. Breeds in the Bichon family are notorious for being difficult and often impossible to completely housetrain. There are theories about why this is true. Some say that resistance to housetraining is a genetic trait, others that the bowels and bladder are very small, so the dog simply cannot wait as long. Regardless of a dog's size, the owner should first try to train the dog as described in the sections below. In some cases, housetraining will go by without a hitch. In others, the dog will seem to be housetrained for a while, but then will revert back to not being reliable. Like all training, housetraining requires patience.

In the case of a small dog that is difficult to housetrain, you might consider a special litter box made for small dogs. These can work very well for the dog and owner. If the dog lives in an apartment, even if the dog is housetrained, some owners prefer using the dog litter box for convenience.

ENSURING A GOOD DIET

No matter what circumstances your dog or puppy came from, the method for housetraining is the same, and begins with transitioning the dog to a high-quality food (see "What Should I Feed My Dog?" in Chapter 4). This transition is critical to successful housetraining, as cheap or low-quality food often acts like a laxative and diuretic, making it almost impossible for a dog to control his bowels and bladder. Give the dog one to two weeks for his body to adjust to any change in diet.

MARKING A DESIGNATED POTTY AREA

Once your dog has adjusted to his new diet, mark a designated area outside that will be the toilet area, where you will train your dog to relieve himself. It may be necessary to put up flagging tape or some other means to identify the area. Marking the area in this way makes it recognizable for the dog. Once your dog goes in his designated area, you can start associating a word or phrase to the action (many people say, "Go potty" or "Do your business"). With practice, when you take your dog to his toilet area and use the term you've chosen, he will know what you want him to do, and where you want him to do it.

Some dogs that have been raised outdoors on concrete or macadam surfaces may refuse to relieve themselves on grass or soil. By the same token, a dog that is used to relieving himself on grass or soil may refuse to go on hard surfaces. If you will be in situations in which your dog will have to relieve himself on unfamiliar surfaces—for instance, if you are going to travel—you should prepare your dog for this. You can teach him to go in different environments simply by taking him there often, especially when he has to relieve himself, so that he learns it is okay to use these surfaces. Typically, a dog will have fewer issues urinating in strange places than moving his bowels.

KEEPING A REGULAR SCHEDULE

Take your dog out on a regular schedule to relieve himself, keeping in mind the general rules of when a dog, especially a young puppy, will feel the need to go:

1. As soon as he wakes up
2. After he plays
3. After he eats
4. Before retiring for the night
5. After being excited

Using your regular schedule, bring the dog to the designated toiled area outside and let him relieve himself. If you are training a puppy, it is necessary to carry him because most young puppies cannot hold it if they walk to the area. As soon as the puppy does his business, give him a treat (or, if you have started clicker training him, a click and then a treat) as well as a hearty "Good boy." For an older dog you can walk him quickly, without letting him sniff around, to the designated area instead of carrying him.

Only play or go for a fun walk after your dog relieves himself, not before. If you play with your dog before he relieves himself, he will hold it as long as possible to get you to play more. If your dog learns to hold it to play longer, in situations where you do not have time to play, you will be forced to wait for him to relieve himself.

HOUSETRAINING AND THE INDOORS

While you are housetraining your dog, do not confine him to a crate to try to force him to hold it when you are gone. This is not fair and will only teach the dog to relieve himself when he is confined, destroying his natural desire to be clean. Instead, block off an area of a room, such as a kitchen, bathroom, or laundry room where the dog's crate, food, water, and toys can be located. The size of this area will depend upon how large the dog is: it should be large enough that the dog could relieve himself and still have plenty of clean space that he can use to move away from his urine or feces. You can put newspapers or another type of material down for the dog to use as his indoor toilet area. This provides a safe area for the dog in the event that he cannot wait for you to take him out, or if you are away all day.

Once your dog is reliably housetrained, you can take up the potty papers and barrier used to block his access to the rest of the house. Some dogs get used to using the papers and you may have to move them close to the door and then outside to help the dog make the transition. When the transition has been made, keep an eye on your dog even if he has not had an accident in the house. Some dogs take up to six months or longer to become fully reliable. This is especially true for dogs that have to stay alone during the day while you are at work. Most dogs are able to wait up to eight hours before they cannot wait any longer, but if the dog is going to be left alone for more than six hours, it would be a good idea to have someone come at some point during the day and walk your dog.

YOUR DOG WILL TELL YOU WHEN HE HAS TO GO

Watch your dog for signs that he has to go out. They know when they have to go, and they will find a way to tell you. Many dogs will whine, but they may also use body language. I am severely hearing impaired and even with hearing aids often cannot hear my dogs if they whine to go out. All of my animals, both dogs and cats, have learned to hit me or otherwise make physical contact with me to let me know what they want—something I did not have to teach them. So, watch carefully for your dog's own way of telling you, give your dog credit for figuring out how to let you know, and always reward the signal that you want to reinforce.

You can also teach your dog to ring a bell by the door to let you know when he has to go out. Simply hang the bell by the door and when you know the dog has to go out, wait until he accidently hits the bell, click and treat him and then take him out. He will learn quickly that by ringing the bell you will come to let him out.

Be careful when using the bell technique with large dogs, especially if they tend to hit the bell with their paw. Some dogs have been known to get so excited that they slam the bell and send it flying across the room or badly scratch the door with their nails. To avoid this, only click the dog for hitting the bell with his nose.

Another word of caution: some dogs seem to enjoy making you come running at their whim! They may ring the bell to get you to take them out to play or for other reasons. They may, for instance, be thinking, "Look, there's a squirrel out there!" (I have certainly had some of my dogs try that on me.) To solve this issue, ask the dog, "Do you have to go potty?" (or whatever word you use with your dog). If the dog stands and looks at you, he most likely does not have to relieve himself. If he gets excited and runs to the door, he has to go. If you only take him out when he has to go and not every time he wants to go outside, your dog will learn to only alert you if he has to go.

ACCIDENTS AND CLEAN-UP

If your dog has an accident in the house, do not scold him. As we have seen (Chapter 3), the old method of showing the dog what he did and then scolding him does not work! After all, except for his desire to keep clean and be able to

Never act upset if your dog has an accident. If the dog experiences stress or associates stress with relieving himself, it will make housetraining more difficult.

get away from his toilet area, dogs are not repelled by their own feces, or anyone else's. Urine and feces are a form of marking to a dog: dogs sniff and sometimes eat other dogs' and animals' droppings regularly. By sticking the dog's nose in or near his feces or urine, all you are doing is showing the dog that he left you a present. To the dog, you are not saying, "Look what you did!" but simply, "Look, you were here."

Do not let the dog see you clean up the mess—it only draws attention to it, and some dogs like the acknowledgment. Be sure to use a product that kills the bacteria as well as the odor (and note that any live bacteria will cause an odor that the dog can smell, even if you cannot smell it). There are many widely accessibly cleaning products that work well.

First, wipe or sop up the wet area. If a carpet is involved, be sure to soak the carpet to the pad if the urine went that deep. Soak the liquid up with old towels or paper towels until you get most of it. Next you must neutralize the urine left on the floor or in the carpet. One old standby is a mixture of one part white vinegar and three parts water. Pour or spray this mixture on the carpet and let it soak in, then sop as much up as you can with old towels or paper towels. Next, sprinkle baking soda on the carpet; it will turn yellow until all the liquid has been soaked up. Keep adding baking soda until it stays white and dry on the top. When it stays white, leave it there for an hour or so to be sure all of the liquid has been absorbed, then shovel up the baking soda and toss it. There will be a white residue on the carpet, but once it thoroughly dries it is easy to vacuum up and your carpet will look like new. In my experience, this works on most carpets. That being said, be sure to spot-test your carpet first, just in case.

Crate Training

For a number of reasons, it is important that every dog is comfortable being in a crate. The crate not only keeps people and objects safe from the dog, but also keeps the dog safe from potentially dangerous situations and objects. There are also situations in which your dog may be required to be in a crate, such as when you are traveling by plane. A crate may also be the best way to transport your dog in other situations, such as going on road trips or attending sports. In the context of SAR, there are situations in which dogs may have to wait in a staging area until they are assigned to work; the safest way to leave them is in a crate. Even at home, there are circumstances in which it is best for the dog to be in a crate. For instance, a puppy may initially be upset at being taken away from his litter and mother, and cry when first brought home. In this case, you can keep him in a crate near your bed at night so he doesn't feel alone.

At first, some dogs may not like their crate. If the dog is introduced to the crate incorrectly, being in the crate may even cause him fear or anxiety. But if care is taken in selecting a crate, and crate training is done correctly (this includes never using the crate to punish your dog), any dog can learn to feel comfortable in his crate. The crate should be his safe place.

CHOOSING YOUR CRATE

Care should be taken to choose a crate that your dog will feel comfortable in. The crate you choose must be big enough for the grown dog to stand up, turn around, and stretch out. The crate needs a soft bed for the dog to sleep on, and water and food bowls as needed. I have found that the large cups made for large bird cages work very well as water and food cups in a wire crate. They attach easily to the wire, cannot be knocked over, and can be positioned at any height or location that suits the situation. The cups easily twist off the holder, making them easy to clean and refill.

Photo 5.1 Even a cat can be taught to enjoy being in a crate! Note the cup attached to the side of the crate to hold water. In this photo my cat, Melfi (also known as MiMi) is snoozing in my dog Riley's crate.

The cage-type crate is my preferred crate type for a number of reasons. In a cage crate, the dog can have full air circulation in hot weather and the dog can see out in all directions. This way the dog is not in a situation in which he can hear and smell something approaching and without being able to see it. Cage crates can, however, also be covered, making them warmer in cold weather and acceptable for air travel. They also fold down into a suitcase-like configuration, making them easier to store, carry, and maneuver.

GETTING YOUR DOG TO LIKE HIS CRATE

Feed your dog in his crate and make it fun for him to go in there by, for instance, giving him Kong toys stuffed with treats. To get your dog used to the crate, you can toss a treat in and, telling your dog he is a good boy, let him go in, get the treat, and come out again. Do not close the door of the crate at this point. As the dog becomes comfortable going in and out of the crate, you can give him a treat, close the door for a few seconds, then open it and let the dog out.

Once your dog is crate trained, leave the crate set up and opened so that your dog can go there to relax. If the crate contains a nice soft bed and is in a location where the dog feels safe, your dog will go into the crate on his own when he feels the need to get away, rest, or simply hang out.

WHEN NOT TO USE THE CRATE

While a crate can be a handy tool for some circumstances at home, it should not be used for long periods of time during the day. Be sure to never leave your dog in his crate for more than two to three hours at a time. Young puppies must be kept in the crate for even shorter periods since they cannot control their bowls or bladder for long periods of time. If you have to leave your dog alone during the day and he is not yet trained well enough to have free run of the house without getting into mischief, confine him to a puppy-proof room rather than a crate all day.

As well, a crate should not be used to housetrain a puppy or to re-train an adult dog. Using a crate in this way often causes a puppy or dog to dislike the crate because he will feel uncomfortable in it if he needs to relieve himself—and if he cannot hold it until you take him out, you are forcing your dog to lie near his "accident," which will undo housetraining.

Finally, the crate should never be used as punishment. Do not grab the dog, scold him, and then put him in his crate. You can put a dog that is very excited in his crate to calm down, but your attitude in this case should be one of understanding rather than anger. If a dog associates the crate with your being angry with him, he will develop a dislike for the crate.

———

While not part of formal obedience training, housetraining and crate training are important for your dog's comfort and safety—and for keeping your house clean and tidy! Chapter 6—the final chapter on pre-training basics—will go over another important comfort and safety issue: handling your dog's body, specifically in the context of grooming.

6

Handling Your Dog's Body for Grooming and Hygiene

Teaching your dog to allow his body and body parts to be handled is useful not only for day-to-day grooming and hygiene, but also for dental and veterinary procedures.

A dog that is used to having his body handled will

- be less stressed during general care and veterinary visits;
- be easier to treat in the event of an injury;
- better tolerate the administration of medications;
- be easier to groom; and
- be less likely to react negatively when encountering children.

A dog that is used to being handled also tends to be more relaxed around children, who often play with dogs by touching the dogs' paws and ears, or grabbing their fur. If you have children in your life, keep in mind that small children should be taught to ask before they play with any dog, whether the child knows the dog or not. This includes your dog, even if the dog is used to being handled. Parents should never allow a young child to have unsupervised, free access to any dog.[1]

In this chapter, you will find tips on how to introduce your dog to being handled, as well as to the tools you may use while grooming him. Tips specific to certain body parts are found in the first section; more general grooming tips, as well as information about bathing and hair care, are found in the second section.

Handling Your Dog's Body

The best time to get a dog used to having his body handled is when he is a puppy. However, with patience you can get the adult dog to at least tolerate being handled. It is good practice to teach your dog the name

Toddlers should never be allowed to be around any pet unsupervised, and should only have access to the pet if he is known to tolerate very small children. Older children should also be supervised, even if they understand the rules for playing with a dog. It is a judgment call on the part of the adults as to when a child is responsible enough to be alone with a pet.

of each part of the body that you plan to touch, and to name it when you are about to touch it so the dog will understand where he will be touched. You can, for example, say something like, "Give me your foot." (I use the word *foot* instead of *paw* since the command *give me your paw* is often the same command used to teach your dog to shake hands.) Using a different word lets the dog know what you plan to do so he can mentally prepare. Note, too, that in the case of grooming, you will have to get your dog comfortable not only with you touching him in certain ways, but also with the various grooming tools you will use.

MOUTH AND TEETH
When teaching a young, teething puppy (up to six months old) to allow you to handle his mouth, keep in mind that teething is uncomfortable and could be painful for the puppy, so you must be especially gentle. After each step in handling your dog's mouth, be sure to give him a click, a treat, or both. If you handle a puppy's mouth roughly and cause pain, he may not like his mouth being handled for the rest of his life.

Even if there was no rough handling in the past, some dogs do not like having their mouth restrained. You may have to begin by merely holding your dog's snout as if you were going to open his mouth. Getting your dog used to having his mouth restrained and held will make it easier to give him oral medications. Being able to open your dog's mouth and examine his teeth will allow you to notice dental problems, brush his teeth, and make him more relaxed during visits to the veterinarian. Working dogs especially will often break the tips of their canines. By regularly checking their teeth, you will be aware of this sooner rather than later. If you do notice a broken tooth, mention it to your veterinarian so it can be monitored; usually no repair is necessary unless the dog seems uncomfortable.

Photo 6.1 Matt teaches Grady how to allow him to examine his teeth. The best way to handle the dog's muzzle is with one hand under the dog's chin and the other on top to lift the dog's lips for dental examination.

It is important that your hands are clean and that you do not have anything on your hands that may make them smell or taste bad for your dog. (Some dogs, for example, do not like the smell or taste of hand lotion.) You might even make your hands smell nice for the dog by rubbing them with something the dog likes, such as peanut butter. You don't need much; since dogs have an excellent sense of smell, a little works just fine. Once your dog is used to having his mouth handled, you do not have to intentionally scent your hands, but do always be sure that they will not smell or taste offensive to the dog.

Start by lifting the dog's lips to look at his teeth. Gently lift his right lip, then praise him and give him a treat. Then do the same with the left lip. Do not do this more than two times in a session. You can do a few sessions per day, but be careful not to overdo it.

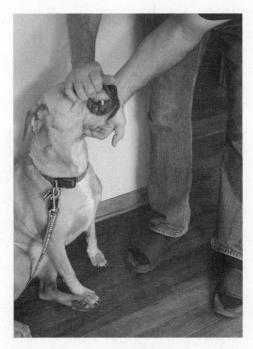

Photo 6.2 Kevin holds Sunny's lip up to examine his teeth.

You will know when your dog is comfortable with you lifting his lips, because he will not shake his head or pull back. When your dog gets to this point, you can lift the lip and then gently run your finger over his front teeth, stopping at the canines. Touch both the upper and lower front teeth. Praise your dog and give him a treat, and repeat this until he is comfortable, just like you did to get him comfortable lifting his lip.

When he is comfortable with you touching his teeth, you can run your finger to the back of his mouth to the last molar. You may have to run your finger on his gums as well as his teeth. Don't rush this process by trying to do both the upper and lower teeth all at once. First, run your fingers along the upper teeth on both sides, and then let your dog relax before doing the lower teeth.

FEET

Many dogs hate having their feet touched. I don't know of any scientific studies that have looked into it, but I suspect that some dog's feet are more sensitive than others. Still, even though some dogs might not like it, they must learn to tolerate it. Handling your dog's feet is necessary for your dog's well-being, as it is required for clipping your dog's nails; trimming hair on the feet and between the toes, which easily gets dirty and may affect traction; and removing seeds, burs, ice (in some climates), and other objects that might get stuck between your dog's toes. The ability to clean your dog's feet may also cut down on housecleaning: if a dog has long hair, his owner may want to keep the hair around the dog's feet trimmed so he does not track mud into the house. For more information on hair trimming, see the section on the subject later in this chapter.

Because it is easy to poke a dog when you are trying to trim hair around his feet (or remove a matt close to his skin or any sensitive area), it is best to use a pair of blunt-nosed grooming scissors so you do not poke him with something sharp.

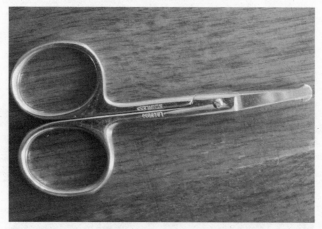

Photo 6.3 An example of blunt-nosed grooming scissors.

Photo 6.4 Babs is taught to allow her paw and toes to be handled. Remember, you must do this with each paw and all toes.

For both a puppy and adult dog, you can start by massaging his feet as a way of caressing him. Each time you handle your dog's feet, be sure to give him a click, treat, or both for letting you do it, even if he is not delighted with the handling. When

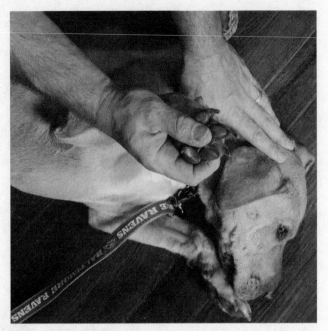

Photo 6.5 Sometimes it is easier to have your dog lie down while you handle his paws, as Kevin illustrates with Sunny.

your dog accepts this (and maybe even enjoys it!) start gently handling his toes. Rub each toe top, bottom, and in-between. If the dog is unsure of this type of handling, only do one or two toes in a session. Be sure to give the dog a treat or click after you handle each toe. Start with short sessions, often throughout the day.

TAIL AND RUMP

Just as some dogs do not like their feet handled, some do not like having their tails or the rump area touched, but you will need to get your dog to at least tolerate being handled here. For dogs with longer coats, it may be necessary to trim the hair around their anus to keep them clean. Some dogs also need the hair on their front and back legs (sometimes referred to as "feathers") trimmed to keep it clean. Teaching your dog to be comfortable with handling of his tail and rump will also make him more accepting of any ministrations that may be needed, such as having his temperature taken during a routine veterinarian visit.

Using the same technique as was used to accustom your dog to having his feet handled, gently massage the tail and the sensitive areas of the rump. You may have to start by manipulating the tail so that you can move it to trim hair.

Photo 6.6 Jade illustrates with Grady how to teach your dog to allow you to handle his tail. She touches Grady's back to make him feel more comfortable having his tail handled.

Photo 6.7 Kevin gently holds Sunny's side to steady him while handling his tail. Sometimes this is necessary to clean a dog's rump area.

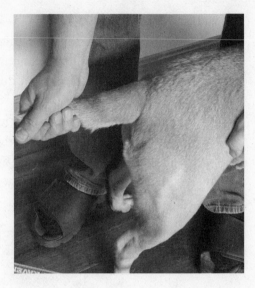

EARS

Most dogs do not mind having their ears handled because owners typically touch their dogs' ears as a form of affection.

Some dogs build up wax in their ears faster than others. Other dogs—particularly those with long ears (such as spaniels and hounds) and those that go into water or frequently get their ears wet—are more prone to ear infections than others. Hot, humid weather can also contribute to an ear infection.

In these cases, you will have to clean your dog's ears. When cleaning ears, do not go deep with a cotton swab; rather, use a soft cloth or cotton ball and your finger. Especially for dogs prone to infection, you should regularly use an ear cleanser to prevent infection. I have found that the DermaPet products work best, though your veterinarian may recommend other products that also work. For the best results, use the ear cleanser after the dog gets wet and after a bath. It is also important to

Photo 6.8 Matt is examining Grady's ears to get him used to having his ears handled.

check your dog's ears (and the rest of his body) after he has been outdoors anywhere with brush, weeds, and other debris since he may get that debris in his ears or caught on the hair around the ears.

Even with thorough ear hygiene practices, infections may occur. The first sign of an infection is a change in the odor: even if you cannot see any sign of an infection because it is too deep in the ear, you will smell it. For this reason, it is important to learn what your dog's healthy ear smells like. Other signs of ear infection include your dog rubbing his ears on the floor, shaking his head frequently, scratching his head or ears often, or crying when he scratches the area around his ears. If you see these behaviors, take your dog to the veterinarian right away.

Photo 6.9 Sometimes a dog will relax more if he is lying down. In this photo Kevin is examining Sunny's ears. Most dogs like to have their ears rubbed, and may even go to sleep if you rub their ears. Sunny is just about asleep.

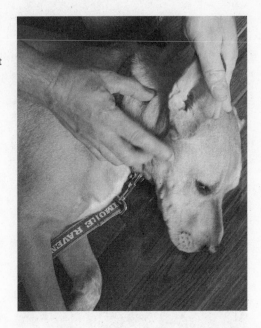

Notes on Grooming

Grooming is important to your dog's health and well-being. Making it a smooth and easy process for you and your dog requires that you teach him to have his body parts handled comfortably. If you are going to take on all of your dog's grooming yourself, it is also essential for your dog's comfort that you use the correct equipment the way it was intended to be used. This includes brushes, combs, nail clippers, scissors or electric hair clippers, blow driers, and even the bath. This section will go over what to keep in mind when grooming your dog, and how to use your equipment.

You may, however, decide not to groom your dog yourself, in which case you should look for a professional groomer that has been highly recommended. A groomer is a good option for dogs that have thick coats and are not easy to groom or bathe, for anyone who is not fond of bathing their dog in their bathtub, for dogs that hate the bath so much that the owner is not able to hold the dog in the bathtub long enough to give the dog a proper bath, and for owners who are not comfortable using electric clippers to keep their dog's coats neat.

Remember, however, that if you have not taught your dog to like having his body parts handled, or if your dog has not responded positively to being conditioned to having his body parts handled, he may not like going to the groomers. Do not automatically assume that a dog's negative reaction about going to the groomer is a sign that the groomer has frightened or hurt your dog. At one point in my life, I was a groomer myself and witnessed many an uncooperative dog mope throughout a whole grooming session— but they certainly weren't hurt. Usually, their attitude completely changed when their owner came in: they would prance around, proud of their new haircut, showing off as if they did it themselves. What characters dogs can be!

Regardless, be sure to ask around and get recommendations. You want a groomer who is kind and does not use force to groom your dog. Almost all groomers will, however, use a restraint to keep your dog from jumping off the grooming table and possibly getting hurt. If your dog tries to nip the groomer, he or she may also use a muzzle. A good groomer should not use any other methods to restrain your dog.

THE WEEKLY GROOMING AT HOME

A weekly grooming provides a special bonding opportunity for you and your dog and goes a long way to keeping your dog happy and healthy. Grooming your dog once a week is one of the best ways to prevent problems, and to catch those that do occur early.

Weekly grooming should involve the following:

1. Carefully brushing your dog to remove mats and look for parasites

2. Checking on your dog's general hygiene to see if he has developed doggie body odor or rolled in something that was not initially obvious and needs to be freshened up (there are special wipes designed for this) or have a bath

3. Brushing your dog's teeth (ideally this will be done daily)

4. Clipping your dog's nails

You should also regularly run your hands over the dog's body to feel for lumps. To the dog, this is like getting a massage treatment. More than feeling nice, though, it is important to do. As your dog ages, it is more likely that he will develop fatty tumors. Any lumps that are not a result of an insect sting should be brought to the attention of your veterinarian. Just like you, your dog's lumps can be cancerous.

The amount of time a grooming session will take depends on the type of coat your dog has. Dogs with longer, silkier coats tend to develop mats in their coats. Mats behind the ears can be especially painful since they can form close to the skin and pull when the dog moves or scratches himself, which feels the same as someone pulling your hair. If you notice that your dog cries when he scratches his ears, check for mats. If you find none, you are probably dealing with an infection (see *Ears*, above).

> For most dogs, grooming will be enjoyable if they are rewarded when being handled and are not hurt while being groomed.

BRUSHING AND BRUSHES, COMBING AND COMBS

Giving your dog a once-over with a brush and/or comb will prevent mats from forming and remove debris. Even with short-haired dogs, a careful brushing will help you see if your dog has any parasites such as ticks and fleas and will help you spot any abrasions or cuts. In some cases, if your dog has gotten

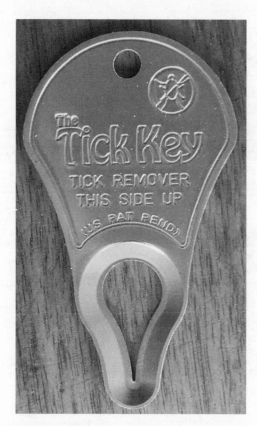

Photo 6.10 If you live in an area where there are ticks, the Tick Key and other similar products work very well to remove ticks on dogs, other pets, and people.

tapeworms or roundworms, you may see worm segments, or the worms themselves, by his anus. If your dog is prone to hot spots or other skin rashes, you will also be able to see these before they get too bad.

Combs are useful for both untangling and removing undercoat. A comb that I like is the Untangler. It tends to pull less on the dog's coat because the teeth rotate and have some give. It also has blunt teeth that are less likely to scratch your dog. Other combs can be sharp and hurt the dog's skin. Regardless of the brush or comb you use, it is always best practice to use it carefully in order to protect your dog's skin.

Photo 6.11 The Untangler comb has blunt teeth that rotate and recess a little to follow the contour of the dog's skin. Note that the middle teeth of the comb are recessed.

Photo 6.12 The two types of bristle brushes. The light colored one is very soft and the dark colored one is stiffer, but not so stiff that the bristles do not give when brushing your dog.

For day-to-day brushing, there are two main types of bristle brushes: soft-bristle brushes and stiff-bristle brushes. Soft-bristle brushes can be used to "finish" the dog's coat. They will remove all loose hair easily without hurting the dog. If your dog has a short coat, you should only use a soft-bristle brush; combs are not necessary. You can use a brush with stiffer bristles on a medium- to long-haired dog. When choosing a brush, be sure to run it over your hand or arm to see how stiff the bristles are. Also note that some brushes have synthetic bristles and others have natural bristles. The brush you choose will depend on your preference and what works best for your dog's coat.

If your dog has a dense undercoat, regular brushes and combs may not remove the undercoat easily. If this is the case with your dog, you can try a specialized brush made for removing under-coat. Many people turn to shedding blades to remove their dog's undercoat, but I don't recommend these because, if used with too much pressure, they can hurt your dog's skin. Instead, try one of the many deshedding brushes or curry combs available. These are brushes and combs with thick fingers that are designed to remove the dog's undercoat. Dogs usually like this type of brush/comb since the thick, finger-like bristles are firm but pliable, giving the dog a massage as you brush. Another good product to remove undercoat is a Furminator comb (Photo 6.13). It may not look like

Photo 6.13 The Furminator is great for dogs as well as cats and other furry pets.

it will work, but I can personally attest that it does—and well—though you must still be careful not to scratch the dog's skin.

Another common type of brush used in grooming, called a slicker brush, has small metal bristles made of thin wire that are bent on the ends. Many people use the slicker brush to try to remove their dog's undercoat, but this is an incorrect usage. The slicker brush was designed to be used to fluff dry dogs with curly coats (such as Poodles) to straighten out the hair. If used properly, the slicker brush never touches the dog's skin and is used with a blow dryer. If you dig into a dog's coat with a slicker brush, you can cut or scratch the surface of his skin. This, of course, hurts the dog, and can cause him to dislike being groomed.

Another important type of comb to have on hand is a flea comb, which is used to look for fleas and flea droppings. Typically, you will run the flea comb along the top of the dog's hind quarters.

Photo 6.14 Slicker brushes like the one pictured above should only be used by a groomer. They are not intended to brush out a dog's undercoat.

If you do find little black specks, collect a few and put them in a single drop of water. If they are flea droppings, they will turn red—flea droppings are largely made of blood.

If you do find flea droppings, it means your dog has a fair number of fleas and needs to be treated. Talk to your veterinarian about controlling fleas; there are products that you can get from your veterinarian that work much better than store-bought products. Keep in mind that if your dog has had fleas for even a single week, it is more than likely that you are also dealing with a flea infestation in your house, especially where the dog sleeps. You will have to treat the house as well in order to completely resolve the problem.

Photo 6.15 An example of a flea comb. Every dog owner should have one, as they are not only excellent for finding fleas or flea droppings but also can be used to remove small seeds and sticks that may get caught in your dog's coat.

HAIR AND HAIR TRIMMING

If you will need to trim your dog's hair, start by handling the hair with your fingers: move it, run your fingers through it, and even gently hold the hair in the same manner that you will to trim the hair. Each time you do this, give your dog a click, a treat, or both.

When you can touch the areas that you need to trim, introduce the scissors or clippers by letting the dog sniff them and by touching the dog with them. If you are using electric clippers, you may have to get your dog used to the sound and vibration of the clippers before you use them. Start by turning the clippers on, making sure they are not too close to your dog. Act happy and reward your dog so that he associates the sound of the clippers as a signal for a reward. When he does not show concern over the sound of the clippers, you can touch his body briefly with the clippers, rewarding him when you remove them. Do this until the dog does not mind being touched with the clippers. Once he is okay with that, you can start gently clipping his hair.

Periodically check your clippers to be sure that they are not too hot—they can get hot enough to become painful. Your local pet shop should have spray made for clippers that can cool them when they get too hot.

If you are using scissors, I find that the best choice is a blunt-ended pair of grooming scissors since you cannot accidently poke your dog if he moves. This is especially true when trimming between the dog's toes. Your scissors should, however, be sharp so they do not pull the dog's hair when you snip.

Be sure that if you are using scissors to trim sensitive areas, or if your dog's hair is long and/or thick, that you hold the hair at the base between your fingers so that you do not cut the dog. Extreme care must be taken if you need to trim around a dog's ears, either with scissors or clippers, because it is very easy to cut or even cut off a dog's ear. The best way to ensure that you do not cut the dog's ear is to feel where the ear flap is, hold the ear flap between your fingers, and use your fingers as a barrier between your scissors and the ear. Only cut hair that protrudes from between your fingers.

Patience is the word when letting your dog get used to this type of handling. Because you are using tools that are sharp and could hurt your dog, it is important that you are able to handle your dog's body and trim his hair without him startling. With patience and care, it is not difficult to keep your dog safe when trimming his hair.

BRUSHING TEETH

Wait until your dog is okay having his snout held while you run your finger over his gums and teeth before you introduce a toothbrush or fingerbrush made for dogs. If you have a puppy, you should also wait until all of the baby teeth have fallen out, the adult teeth have grown in, and you are sure your dog does not have sore gums.

When your dog is comfortable with this, you can add canine toothpaste. Only use toothpaste or gel made for dogs as human toothpaste is toxic to dogs. It will take a bit of time for the dog to get used to having the toothpaste in his mouth. Some dogs try to eat the paste, making it difficult to brush their teeth, but with patience it can be done. I have found that the tooth gel made by DermaPet works the best for me. Try different brands to see what your dog likes.

Ideally you should brush your dog's teeth once a day. If you cannot brush your dog's teeth every day, you should do it at least once a week. Although dogs generally do not get cavities like people do, keeping your dog's teeth and gums clean will avoid gum diseases and the loss of teeth when he gets older.

Every dog, like every person, will have a different chemical make-up in his saliva that causes him to build up tartar and plaque at different rates. Therefore, some dogs need to have their teeth cleaned professionally as often as every six months, while other dogs can go for years without tartar build up. Your veterinarian will check your dog's teeth during his yearly visit, but unless you regularly check your dog's mouth, you will not know how much professional dental care your dog actually needs.

If you notice a foul odor, caked-on yellow or brown gunk at the base of the teeth, or inflamed gums, you should take your dog to the veterinarian right away. These are signs of gum disease and infections, which are not only uncomfortable for your dog, but can even be fatal. A dog that has heart issues can die from gum disease–related complications.[2]

TRIMMING NAILS

It is important that your dog let you clip his nails as soon as possible, as the nails on most dogs grow fairly quickly. If the dog does not engage in activities that keep them worn down, you may have to cut your dog's nails as often as once a week. Cutting your dog's nails is important to keep the quick from growing too long—if that happens, you will need to have your veterinarian trim your dog's nails for you.

When your dog allows you to handle his feet and toes, start holding the paw as you would to clip his nails without actually clipping his nails. Sometimes this means pushing hair away from the nail so that you can see it, and separating each toe for better access.

When it comes time to clip the nails (that is, when your dog is comfortable with the previous step), be sure that you identify where the quick (the pink area) ends in his nail. For dogs with black nails you will have to estimate. There are several different methods of estimating the quick,[3] but if you have trouble determining this, go to a groomer or your veterinarian and let them show you. They will be able to determine where the quick is and demonstrate how to find it better than a written explanation or general diagram can show you.

It is painful if you cut the quick in your dog's nail, so, particularly as your dog is getting comfortable with you cutting his nails, do not cut large pieces of nail right away. Start instead by frequently clipping only the tips of the nails in order to gradually work the nail back. Be sure to give your dog a treat after clipping each nail and work slowly, paying attention to how your dog reacts. This way you can be sure not to hurt your dog.

In case of an accident, however, it is important to have styptic powder or gel on hand to help stop bleeding. I prefer the gel since the powder is moisture sensitive and over time can harden in its container.

If your dog absolutely will not tolerate having his nails clipped using this method, there is a last-resort method that works most of the time. You will need someone to help you do this. Get a jar of meat-based baby food and have your assistant hold the jar in his hand in such a way that his fingers block the opening of the jar, leaving about one inch of space. Let the dog try to lick the baby food while you trim a nail. Most dogs are so focused on the food that they will tolerate the nail trimming—and, as a bonus, it also rewards him for letting you do it!

NAIL CLIPPERS

You can trim your dog's nails by using clippers or a grinder. There are many different brands of clippers and grinders. The method you use will depend on what you feel comfortable handling and what your dog will tolerate.

There are two basic types of nail clippers: the scissor type and the guillotine type. The scissor type cuts the nail from both sides, the same as any pair of scissors. The guillotine type has a blade that slides down and cuts from either the top or bottom of the nail, depending on which way you hold the clipper.

Most professionals use the scissor-type nail clippers, which seem to stay sharper longer. The guillotine type has a thin blade and I personally have found that they get dull quickly. It is important that your nail clipper is sharp because dull nail clippers will be

> Be sure your nail clippers are sharp. Dull nail clippers can hurt a dog.

uncomfortable for the dog, making him dislike having his nails clipped.

If you choose not to use clippers to trim your dog's nails, you may use a hand-held electric grinder with a grinding bit made for dogs. Dremel tools can work well, but you can purchase a purpose-made dog nail grinder. Some dogs will not tolerate nail grinders and others will. If your dog doesn't mind this method, and you can use the grinder correctly without grinding the quick of the nail, it does give a smoother finish to the nail. If you use a clipper and want a smoother finish, you can also file the edges of the dog's nails with a dog nail file.

THE BATH

The two times a year at which every dog should be bathed are the spring and fall, because the bath will help loosen and remove shedding hair. Besides these two times, the frequency at which you bathe your dog depends on what your dog does and the type of coat he has. Dogs that have oilier coats—usually those that have been bred to work in water—may develop a "doggie" odor more often. Working dogs, or any dog that is active outdoors, may become very dirty and may need a bath when they are finished with their job or other vigorous activity.

There are a few techniques for giving a dog a bath that make it more enjoyable for the dog. That being said, I have never personally met a dog that really *loves* a bath. Even the dog that thoroughly enjoys splashing and wallowing in a muddy puddle, or loves going for a swim, gets mopey when you replace his puddle or lake with soap and clean water.

If your dog absolutely hates a bath, you can do a few things to get him to accept it. First and foremost, make sure that you use a non-slip bath mat. Some dogs fear a bath because they cannot maintain their footing. Next be sure that the water is not too hot or too cold. Warm water is best. Next you can practice placing the dog in the bathtub, or wherever you plan on bathing your dog. Simply put him in that place, reward him, and then let him out right away. As he gets comfortable, you can increase the time he stays in the bathing place. Once he is okay being there, you can run warm water in the bathtub (not *on* the dog), letting the water touch his feet. When he is okay with that, gently pour water over his rump.

In general, dogs tend to not mind water on their body but do mind it in their face, so get the dog used to the bath without getting his face wet; save the face-washing for the actual bath.

When bathing your dog, it is important to use shampoo made specifically for dogs. Some are even supposed to be mild enough that they won't hurt the dog if they get in his eyes. For dogs that need to bathe more frequently, consider using a conditioner specifically made for dogs to help restore their coat.

Start by wetting the dog with warm water, making sure not to pour water directly on the face. Use a cloth or sponge to wet, soap, and rinse the dog's face, keeping water and soap out of your dog's ears, eyes, and nose. Rinse the soap from the dog's face using the sponge or rag to help control where the water goes. For some dogs, holding their nose to the ceiling lets the water run to the back of their head instead of in their eyes, ears, and nostrils.

Once the dog's head is washed, you can soap the rest of his body. Start from the back of the head and work to the tail. If the dog has fleas, this will keep them from going into the dog's eyes, nose, and ears. Note, too, that regular dog shampoo will kill fleas; you do not need to buy special flea shampoo.

If the dog has a long coat, be sure to scrub the dog's coat with your fingertips so that you wash down to the skin. Once you have accomplished that, you can rinse the dog with clean, warm water, starting from the back of the head and working to the tail. Run your hands through the dog's coat to be sure that you rinse out all of the soap, paying special attention to the belly area.

There are a number of ways to dry your dog after the bath. I always like to towel dry my dogs and then let them lie in the sun or air dry. If your dog has a short coat, you can towel dry him completely. If you dog has a long coat, you may want to blow dry your dog. This will blow out any loose hair and may give your dog a fluffy look. Some dogs do not mind blow drying, but others are terrified of it, so if you plan to blow dry your dog, you must get him used to the blow dryer first by introducing the dryer to him gradually and rewarding him for tolerating it. This will make the process more pleasant for both you and your dog.

Being able to handle your dog's body is important for his hygiene and his overall health, both of which are paramount to having a healthy, happy dog.

Now that you're well versed in the pre-training basics, it's time to move on to obedience training. In Part III of the book, we'll first look at the equipment you will need for training and at how to set up your training environment and routine. Then we'll move on to basic and advanced obedience exercises. Finally, we'll add some fun into the mix and look at a few simple tricks you and your dog can enjoy doing together.

Part III

Basic Obedience Training

7

The Equipment

Understanding the equipment that you need to successfully train a dog is important. It is just as important to use this equipment properly. In this chapter, we will cover the basic equipment—the leash, collar, head harness, and body harness—and how to introduce each piece of equipment to your dog. In general, in order to have your dog accept the training equipment in a positive way, all training equipment must be introduced slowly so the dog does not learn to dislike the equipment. We will also look at the types of equipment not to use.

The chapter will conclude with a look at an important piece of equipment for you—the training log—as well as a brief discussion of toys and how to choose them, and a quick note on clicker training. As this is not a clicker training book, I will not go over the clicker and target stick in detail, but do recommend learning more about these from a trusted resource.

Basic Equipment and How to Use It

THE LEASH
The best leash to use is a single thickness, six-foot-long nylon leash. This type of leash will give you the control you need to properly train your dog. Flexi leashes have become popular, but I

do not recommend ever using a Flexi leash. It does not have the same strength as a regular, six-foot leash, and it is quite simply too flexible. If your dog pulls, he'll go where he wants. This does not give you the control you need for dog training.

It is always a good idea to have at least two leashes so that if you lose, misplace, or break one, you have another immediately available. Also, later in training, you may want to clip two leashes together to create more distance between you and your dog.

Leashes come in a variety of widths: 1-inch, ¾-inch, ½-inch, and ¼-inch. The width of the leash you choose should be determined by the size of your dog. A large dog needs a 1-inch-wide leash and a dog the size of a Yorkshire Terrier might have a ¼-inch-wide leash. Use the size of leash that is strong enough to hold your dog. One way to judge this is by the size of the clip on the end of the leash that is used to attach the leash to your dog's collar, as this is the weakest part of the leash. The narrow, ¼-inch leashes have a smaller, weaker clip that may break if used on a large dog. When in doubt, it is always better to go bigger than smaller.

The clips are usually one of two varieties: slide-bolt (Photo 7.1) and hinge (Photo 7.2). Always choose the slide-bolt and avoid the

Photo 7.1 An example of the slide-bolt clip, the safer variety of clip to have on a leash.

Photo 7.2 The more dangerous hinge-type of clip.

Photo 7.3 To properly hold the leash, put the loop (handle) around your right-hand thumb.

hinge varieties, as it is possible for the hinge to get caught on the pad of your dog's foot or between his toes. If this happens, you will have to take the dog to the veterinarian to have it removed and the dog will be in pain until it is taken off.

USING THE LEASH

The leash is held in your right hand. Open your hand and place the loop end of the leash over your thumb, allowing the leash to fall across your palm. Close your hand over the leash, making a fist. Do not put the loop over your wrist. If the loop is around your wrist, your dog can pull the leash off your hand.

You can take up the slack in the leash by looping it into (not around) your fist. Do not use your left hand to hold the leash as you will need your left hand to work with the dog during training.

THE COLLAR

The everyday collar should be a martingale-type of collar that is made of flat nylon. You can adjust this type of collar so it is tight enough to prevent the dog from backing out of it if he becomes frightened or very stubborn, yet is loose and comfortable around the dog's neck when he wears it around the house.

Photo 7.4 An example of a martingale collar. Note the small loop that goes through the two D-rings, one of which holds the ID tags.

The small loop on the martingale-type collar is where the leash is attached, and it provides a handle if you have to hold your dog and do not have a leash handy. The small loop goes through two D-rings, to which you can attach the dog's ID tags.

In some cases, you can use a flat buckle collar. Some people feel that a flat buckle collar is better to have on your dog if the dog is crated or in a situation where the martingale collar may become caught on something.

In situations where the dog is working and his collar might get caught on brush or other hazards in the environment, you may not want your dog to wear a collar at all. When the dog is in a crate, it is best to have a collar that cannot get caught on anything, or again to have no collar on the dog. However, as soon as your dog is not in a risky situation, you should put the collar back on the dog. If your dog should become lost, even if he is microchipped, the tags on the collar will be the main resource people will use to contact you.

THE HEAD HARNESS

The head harness is very handy to use for some exercises because it allows you to turn the dog's head away from what is distracting him. For very strong dogs, the head harness allows the owner to have control over the dog without using harsh methods. Some people feel that a dog can be injured with a head harness, which is true if the harness is used incorrectly.[1] If properly used, however, it will not injure the dog. More harm is done using chain choke collars, prong collars, and electric collars.

THE BODY HARNESS

There are several designs of body harnesses. Some are designed to keep a dog from pulling, others are supposed to keep a dog from jumping, and still others are simple harnesses used to walk a dog. Some harnesses are padded, some have wider chest and back pieces, and some are simple nylon straps. The best harness for your dog depends on what you want to use it for, as well as the size of the dog and what he likes to wear. This is a decision the owner must make based on his experience with his dog.

I do want to caution that small dogs should always be walked on a standard body harness attached to the leash instead of a neck collar. Although a small dog should wear a neck collar that has identification tags on it, he should never be walked with a neck collar of any kind as any pressure on the neck collar can damage the dog's trachea and/or neck. However, you can use a head harness, if necessary, for certain exercises, as explained in Chapter 9 and 10.

The harnesses designed to prevent a dog from pulling or jumping should not replace proper training for these issues. If they work at all, they only prevent the problem; they do not teach the dog not to do it.

Photo 7.5 Riley demonstrating a basic type of body harness that is excellent to use with small dogs.

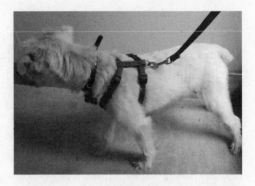

Photo 7.6 A cage muzzle allows the dog to pant, drink, and otherwise open his mouth. It does, however, prevent him from biting. This type of muzzle is often used for sports such as lure coursing or go-to-ground terrier trials.

THE MUZZLE

Some sports require that the dog wear a muzzle, and sometimes a dog must be muzzled so a veterinarian can work on the dog. There are two major types of muzzle: the cage muzzle and the restrictive muzzle. It is a good idea to have your dog get used to wearing a muzzle—both the restrictive and cage variety—so that, if ever there is a situation in which he needs to wear one, he is comfortable doing so.

Photo 7.7 This is an example of a restrictive muzzle. It prevents the dog from biting or opening his mouth at all. It should only be used for very short periods, such as during a veterinarian examination or grooming session where a dog might bite, as the dog will not be able to drink, eat, or pant.

Introducing the Equipment

You cannot train your dog until he is comfortable with the equipment that he will be wearing. The dog will not learn his lessons if he is distracted by his collar, leash, or harness. Therefore, you must take the time to introduce your dog to each piece of equipment you plan to use before you try to train him using them.

> All training equipment must be introduced slowly so the dog does not learn to dislike the equipment.

INTRODUCING THE COLLAR

Typically, a young puppy has not had to wear a collar, so you will have to introduce the collar to the puppy. You can do this once the puppy has adjusted to his new home—usually within a week.

Begin with a standard, flat buckle collar made of softer material to get the puppy used to having something around his neck. It is important to do this before introducing the martingale collar, as the sensation of having a collar that tightens around the puppy's neck may frighten him. Gently put the flat buckle collar on the puppy while being upbeat. Immediately give the puppy a treat and play with him so he does not focus entirely on the collar. Some puppies seem to adjust right away while others do not. Leave the collar on the puppy for 5 to 10 minutes and then take it off, being upbeat the whole time. You can do this a few times a day.

When you notice that the puppy does not seem to mind the collar, you can leave it on for longer periods, up to 15 minutes. Once he is okay with the collar being on for 15 minutes, it should be okay to leave it on all the time.

While it is unlikely that an older dog has not worn a collar, it happens. Some dogs that have been raised in puppy mill environments, for instance, may have never worn a collar. Once the dog has had a few days to adjust to you, introduce the collar the same way you would with a puppy. Some older dogs may accept a body harness rather than a collar. The pressure around the dog's neck from a neck collar may trigger a self-defense reaction in an older dog.

Giving the dog treats while you put the collar on and take it off will help the dog feel better about the collar. Of course, it also helps to keep an upbeat, happy demeanor.

While it is best to get a dog comfortable with his collar before beginning to use a leash, it may be necessary to use a leash right away to walk the dog. Try to do this as gently as possible. Do not drag the dog on the leash; rather lure him to follow you. Be sure to give your dog a treat when he moves with you instead of away from you.

INTRODUCING THE LEASH

Once a puppy or older dog is comfortable with the collar, it is time to introduce the leash. For both puppies and older dogs, start by attaching the leash to the collar. Again, an upbeat, happy attitude helps. Let the dog feel the weight of the leash on his collar while you sit quietly or play with him. It is okay to let the dog drag the leash if it does not frighten him. You do not want to pull on the leash.

Once the dog is comfortable with the leash on his collar, which should only take a day or so, you can pick the leash up and then lure the dog with a treat to follow you. Avoid pulling on the leash. If the dog balks, it is because he is nervous or fearful; stop and let him calm down, then try again. Take just a few steps and then stop and praise the dog. You may at first need to do this in short sessions a few times a day.

Within a few days, the dog should be okay walking on the leash, and you will have started to lay the foundation for future exercises. By being gentle and understanding, you are also building a positive bond with your dog and establishing trust.

INTRODUCING THE MUZZLE

Again, it is a good idea to have your dog get used to wearing both types of muzzles. If your dog is used to wearing one, he will not associate negative feelings with the event or circumstances that require the muzzle. This is especially important for dogs that must be muzzled during veterinarian or grooming visits.

For both puppies and older dogs, introduce the muzzle gradually. I do not recommend introducing a very young puppy or older dog to the muzzle until he is comfortable with the collar and leash.

Start by putting the muzzle on the dog's nose without fastening it, then quickly taking it off. Give the dog a treat before and after. As the dog gets used to the muzzle, you can hold it on his nose for longer periods—a minute or more—before removing it. Once he willingly lets you put it on his nose, you can fasten it for a few seconds before removing it. Continue this process until the dog feels comfortable walking around with a cage muzzle on.

Once the dog is used to the cage muzzle, you can take him for a walk while he wears the muzzle. This way he will not associate anything negative with the muzzle. If the dog is going to wear the muzzle for sporting events (it is, for example, a required piece of equipment in some terrier trials and lure coursing), he will likely begin to look forward to the muzzle. Much like a dog gets excited when you pick up his leash because he knows he is going for a walk, he will learn that his cage muzzle means that fun activities are coming.

Once a dog is used to his cage muzzle, the restrictive muzzle can be slowly introduced in the same fashion. A restrictive muzzle may be needed in a variety of situations in order to keep the dog from biting, including during first aid treatments and, in some cases, grooming. Do not leave a restrictive muzzle on a dog any longer than necessary as it prevents the dog from panting, eating, and drinking.

INTRODUCING THE HEAD HARNESS

Dogs and puppies should be comfortable with the neck collar, body harness, and leash before you introduce the head harness. The head harness is not a muzzle. It does not prevent the dog from biting. Rather, it allows you to control the dog's head position.

It is important to read the use and fit instructions carefully for your particular head harness. If the head harness is not fitted properly, it will be uncomfortable for the dog. All types of head harnesses have a loop that goes over the dog's nose and sits at the bridge of the nose. Dogs that have very short noses or pushed-in (brachycephalic) faces, such as Pugs, Boston Terriers, or English Bulldogs, may need an extra strap that attaches the strap at the back of the neck to the strap on the nose to keep the nose strap in place. Some dogs have noses so short that a head harness cannot be used.

To get the dog used to wearing the head harness, hold the nose loop in your hand so that the loop is open enough for your dog's snout to go through it. Next, hold a treat in front of the loop so your dog has to put his snout through the loop to get the treat. Most dogs will do this quickly at first. As the dog gets the idea of the "game," withhold the treat a little bit longer each time to get him to leave his snout in the loop longer. When he is comfortable with this, gently touch the top of his snout with the loop. Be sure to maintain an upbeat attitude through the whole process.

When you can touch his snout without him backing out of the loop, you can then fasten the harness around the neck. Continue giving your dog treats and praising him for having the head harness on.

Once your dog is comfortable wearing the head harness, attach the leash to the harness and gently lure him to follow you without pulling. Do this for a minute or so, then take the harness off. When your dog is comfortable following you, it is time to use the head harness in training as needed.

Some dogs will fight the head harness and try to pull it off with their paws. Be sure not to let this happen. If the dog learns that he can get the head harness off, it will take longer for him to accept it. If your dog fights the head harness, you need to use baby steps: go through the above steps more slowly. If your dog continues to fight the head harness, try another brand. A different style can make all the difference in the world.

INTRODUCING THE BODY HARNESS

Most dogs do not seem to mind the body harness. However, it is a good idea to introduce it slowly. Let the dog sniff and explore it before putting it on him, all the while giving him treats. Get the dog comfortable wearing the body harness in short increments as you did with the head harness. When the dog is comfortable with the body harness, let him walk around with it on. When he is used to this, attach a leash to the harness and lure him with a treat to follow you. Do not pull on the leash. Once you have practiced this a few times, the next step is to take your dog for a walk with the body harness. As soon as your dog associates a fun walk with the harness, he will be asking you to put it on.

A body harness can be used on young, very small dogs (those about 18 pounds or under), as it is much safer than a collar. I do not, however, recommend using any type of body harness on a young, large dog that is not completely physically mature, as it could put pressure on growing joints and bones and cause damage. For some dogs, maturity is not reached until two years of age. If your dog jumps or pulls so you cannot walk him on a neck collar, use a head harness; it will not injure his joints.

In some cases, using a body harness on a dog may encourage him to pull. This is especially true of sled dog breeds who are bred to pull in a harness. Even though dog sled harnesses are different than those made for everyday use, these dogs still tend to pull. If your dog pulls in a body harness, you may want to use a head harness instead.

Equipment Not to Use

With few exceptions, there is no reason to use chain choke collars, shock collars, or prong collars, even though some trainers promote them. Methods that routinely use these types of equipment are not conducive to a positive relationship with your dog: they focus on pain and punishment rather than positive training. Moreover, most people do not know how to properly use these pieces of equipment and end up abusing them and causing harm to their dogs.

In most cases, shock collars and the like are simply unnecessary: if you properly train your dog, you should not need them. In rare circumstances, however, it may be necessary to use a shock collar. This should only be done by a professional trainer, and only to correct a situation that puts a dog at risk. For example, if you live in an area where you are not allowed to put up a fence, and you cannot trust your dog to stay in your yard off-leash, you may have to resort to an electric fence or an "invisible fence"—an underground wire that, when crossed, transmits a shock to your dog's collar—to keep your dog from running away. That being said, even if you have your dog trained for this type of fence, it is critical that you stay with your dog when he is outside. The electric fence does not keep people or animals from coming into your yard, and if your dog does manage to break through, it will discourage him from coming back afterwards. This is because whatever the dog saw that raised his adrenalin high enough for him to tolerate the shock is not there when he returns, and the dog will not be willing to take the shock again to get back into the yard.

The Journal or Training Log

A training log is a tool that you can use to record your training goals, progress, and failures. The training log will help you remember the details of your session, reminding you what you did, why you did it, and the results that it gave. If you get another dog years later, the training log may help you train your new dog, too. Although every dog is different, it will give you a starting point, reminding you of what worked, what did not, and why.

Below are suggested items to keep in your log. You may wonder why I included the weather. This is because the weather can affect a dog negatively or positively, and can influence how he responds to training on a given day.

TRAINING LOG

1. The dog's information:
   a. Name
   b. Age
   c. Breed
   d. Date of birth
   e. Age spayed/neutered
2. The exercise:
   a. Date
   b. Name of exercise
   c. Weather conditions
   d. Location of training
   e. Method used
   f. Results
   g. What you want to improve
   h. What was unsuccessful (if anything), and why
   i. How you plan to resolve any issues

Toys

Toys are important for a dog because they help him alleviate boredom, expend energy, and, in some cases, vent frustration. You need to make sure you select toys that are safe for your dog.

It is important to consider your dog's chewing habits when selecting a toy. Some dogs have what we call a *soft mouth,* others a *hard mouth.* Retrievers, for instance, are bred to carry game without ruffling the feathers or fur—they have soft mouths. Hard-mouthed dogs, on the other hand, chomp down on anything they can get their mouth on. In general, larger dogs have stronger bites than smaller dogs, but you shouldn't underestimate a small dog's bite.

The best way to select appropriate toys for your dog is to try a variety of toys and see which one your dog both likes and will not destroy. You do not want your dog to destroy toys because the material that they are made of can be harmful to the dog, causing intestinal blockages and other problems if swallowed. Very aggressive chewers will totally demolish most stuffed toys, though there are some cloth toys that are not stuffed, which dogs who like to remove stuffing may play with without ripping to shreds. Other dogs are very gentle with their stuffed toys and will carry them around, sleep with them, and never destroy them. Still other dogs will destroy one type of stuffed toy and not another—for instance, they may not be able to stand having a squeaker in a toy and will not stop until they get the squeaker out, but are otherwise gentle with squeakerless toys.

Selecting a tough toy for your dog doesn't necessarily mean your dog will not be able to tear it to bits. Large, hard-mouthed dogs, and even some small dogs, can easily destroy even tough toys. (My 18-pound Parsons Russell Terrier can destroy Kong products, one of the toughest toys on the market!)

Whichever toy you pick for your dog, you *must* monitor how he plays with it until you are sure he will not destroy it. This means that, while you are still testing toys, your dog only gets the toy when you are there to watch him.

A Note on Clicker Training

Although this is not a book about how to clicker train your dog, a clicker can easily be incorporated into many of the exercises in this book, and I do sometimes mention when to click your dog. Clicker training is a useful tool for communicating with your dog during training. As a bonus, it is fun for the dog and for you. I have taught my dogs some pretty funny tricks using a clicker that would have been difficult to do and taken longer without a clicker. You will do yourself and your dog a favor by learning to use a clicker.

While fun, clicker training must be done properly. The most common challenge people have while learning to use the clicker is understanding that the "click" *is not a command to do anything.*

It only means, "Yes, that is what I want." The advantage to being able to click a "yes" for your dog is that you can do it immediately after your dog gives you the behavior you want. This works in situations where other rewards cannot be given fast enough for the dog to associate the praise with the action (for instance, when you are working at a distance from your dog). Giving your dog a late reward accomplishes little to nothing, as it will reward the dog only for what he was doing or thinking at the moment of the reward. Being able to reward your dog the moment he does what you want makes it easier to shape your dog's behavior and, in many cases, improve and reinforce the behaviors you want to encourage.

A clicker can be purchased at most pet stores. You will also need a target stick, an important tool that teaches the dog *how* to learn with a clicker. You can choose to buy a purpose-made target stick, but they tend to be expensive. A ¼-inch dowel is easily found at most lumber or hardware stores and works just as well. I urge you, too, to get a small, trustworthy booklet that deals with clicker training in more detail, and will help you avoid mistakes. *Getting Started: Clicker Training for Dogs* by Karen Pryor[2] is a very good option, and easy to find. I also recommend *Clicker Training Basics: 7 Insanely Actionable Steps,*[3] an online resource that gives clear, easy instructions for clicker training your dog.

Now that you're set up with the proper equipment, it's time to get your training environment and routine ready—this means finding appropriate, safe spaces in which to train, learning some of the basic dos and don'ts of training, and setting up a schedule that will help you and your dog stay on track. These topics will be dealt with in the next chapter.

8

Setting Up for Success

Many people become upset when their dog disobeys a command that the owner feels the dog should know. This frustration arises, however, because of a lack of understanding of what actually constitutes obedience: obedience is not just learning a command, *but also the ability to exercise the self-control to do it.* It is up to you to give your dog the opportunity to develop self-control. Self-control takes time, and requires that the dog mature mentally, which can take up to a year for some dogs. It also requires practice—and this is not something your dog will do on his own.

It is up to you to guide and work with your dog to develop self-control, and this is why it's important to set up your training sessions in a way that allows your dog to focus, avoids frustrations and learning fatigue, and promotes success.

Train in the Proper Environment

A dog will not and cannot learn if he is in an excitable state. Therefore, you should start your training in an environment where the dog does not have to worry about or be distracted by his surroundings, and can focus on learning his commands. Keep in mind that some dogs can work in a group setting and some cannot. Remember, too, that learning concepts and applying them are two different things. First you must teach the dog the commands; only when he knows them should you ask him to apply them to real-life situations. If you ask your dog to apply what he has not already learned, you are setting your dog up for failure.

As your dog becomes more reliable at his exercises, he can be brought into increasingly distracting environments to practice them, which, if done correctly, will help him develop self-control. All dogs are different, so the amount of time and effort it will take on your part will vary. Be attentive to how well your dog has learned his lessons, and avoid putting your dog in new, busy, or otherwise distracting environments that he is not ready to handle. Some people think that these environments "test" their dogs, or that the dogs will learn to listen better in busy environments. In reality, this can be counterproductive. Dogs are not going to learn quickly if they cannot focus enough to learn. Try teaching a dog or a puppy to *sit-stay* next to a playground full of kids!

> Dogs cannot learn when they are in an excitable state, so learning should take place in a quiet or less distracting environment. Once an exercise is learned, obedience is not a matter of knowing what to do, but the ability to exercise the self-control required to do it.

Train One Concept at a Time

Every specific command you teach your dog can be thought of as a concept. A concept is a clear, coherent idea of something that has been learned. When trained correctly, the dog will be able to apply this idea to new situations that he has not previously encountered in training. A dog can only get to this stage, however, if he is given the freedom to do so: to think and be creative, using what he knows to solve novel problems. And giving your dog this freedom means trusting and nurturing your dog's innate intelligence.

Many people do not realize that dogs can learn very complex concepts if they are taught correctly. Teaching a concept correctly means teaching it in stages. If a dog owner tries to teach his dog more than one thing at a time, it sets the training up for failure. Certainly, some dogs can handle this kind of teaching in a simplified situation, but even in the best case it leaves room for error. For instance, in the *recall*, or *come*, exercise, the dog is required to come toward and sit in front of the person calling him. The dog must therefore combine two separate concepts: sitting on command and coming when called. Trying to teach the dog to sit on command at the same time that you try to teach him to come when called requires the dog to learn two things at once, and that's hard for anyone. But if you teach the dog to sit as a stand-alone exercise, and only then ask him to sit after you call him to come, it is much easier for the dog to learn.

> Dogs can learn concepts if they are taught one step at a time. In order to teach a dog a complex concept, the owner must first understand what a concept is. He must then identify each part or sub-concept that makes up the complete, complex concept in order to be able to show the dog, one step at a time, what he is to learn.

A dog has mastered a concept when he is able to apply it in a new situation. Take the simple example of a dog that has been taught to walk the length of a board. A dog that has been trained in a way that does not cultivate his intelligence may only be able to perform this skill in the specific situation in which it has been trained—that is, he will only be able to walk on certain boards. He may be good at this very specific skill, but he has not mastered the *concept*. A dog that *has* mastered the concept would be able to apply his board-walking skill to other situations, such as walking along a log or other object.

Pattern Training Is a No-No!

People tend to fall into a pattern when they are training their dog. This is something you must consciously think about and avoid doing. Remember, your dog learns by having you show him what to do. If you follow a strict routine, such as always stopping at the same place or after the same number of steps, your dog will think that this pattern is the signal for him to perform a behavior, or is part of what he is supposed to do.

This is not a good thing. When a dog gets used to a pattern, he may not obey you if you break the pattern. The most common example of this is when people teach their dog to sit: almost everyone will start by having the dog sit in front of them. Later, if they must tell their dog to sit when they are in another position, the dog does not respond because he thinks he only has to sit when facing the owner.

> Avoid pattern training. It can lead to confusion for your dog.

Following the training routine as described in this book is not the same as pattern training because each exercise builds on the previous one. I will point out how to avoid pattern training where it applies to the lessons outlined in the next two chapters, including avoiding patterns in where you train, where you stop, and how long you wait to call your dog.

Avoid Learning Fatigue

THE 5-1-5-1-5-QUIT TRAINING FORMULA

To avoid frustration and learning fatigue, try training your dog in 17-minute sessions: three five-minute sessions with two one-minute breaks in between. You will be amazed how much the one-minute breaks help your dog by giving him time to think about what you just did.

You can do 17-minute training sessions as often during the day as you are able, as long as you give the dog at least a half-hour break between each one. Make sure you pay attention to how your dog is responding to the sessions, and use your judgment as to how many sessions your dog can take in a day. As a general rule, the younger the dog, the fewer sessions he should have. Dogs older than 3½ to 4 months can usually handle the full session, but very young puppies may need shorter sessions. You may only want to work with young puppies for five minutes at a time instead of going through the full 5-1-5-1-5 session.

THE 5-1-5-1-5-QUIT TRAINING FORMULA

To help both you and the dog, it is best to use the following formula for training:

1. 5 minutes work
2. 1 minute rest
3. 5 minutes work
4. 1 minute rest
5. 5 minutes work
6. Quit

Wait at least 30 minutes before training again.

It is very important to time your sessions; most people cannot judge how long a minute (or five minutes) really is.

THE START AND END SIGNALS

When you begin training, it is important to teach your dog words or signals that he can associate with the beginning and end of his training sessions. These signals are used simply to help the inexperienced dog differentiate between play and training. Once your dog is fully trained, you may not have to use words for the *start exercise* and *end exercise* signal. Some working dog handlers do, however, always use a word to let the dog know that they are about to start a job.

START EXERCISE SIGNAL

When you first start training your dog, choose a word, any word, to tell the dog that it is time for training—this will be your *start exercise* signal. As you clip the leash on to the dog's collar, you can give him a happy command that he can associate with training. Do not use a common word that everyone else uses in normal conversation. Instead, try to use a specific phrase such as "Let's work," or even a foreign or made up word—it does not matter to the dog! What is important is that you use it consistently at the start of your training sessions.

END EXERCISE SIGNAL

The *end exercise* signal is the more important word connected with the training session.

Picture this scenario: you are working with your dog and he is heeling, staying, and practicing all of his exercises. When it's time to stop, you simply walk away from your dog saying something like, "Good boy." This does not tell the dog anything about the session being over since you should be telling him he is a good boy throughout the training. Instead, as you walk away, you are forcing the dog to determine if he is now free to do what he wants or not. If your dog learns that he can decide when to listen and when not to listen, he may decide in the middle of the exercise that you are finished. Often a dog will resort to reading your body language to make this determination. If your body signals to the dog that training is over when, in reality, it is not, the dog will feel misled or become confused. This can make the trainer angry or frustrated, thinking the dog has disobeyed when in reality he was trying to do what he thought you wanted.

With this in mind, simply choose another word that is not commonly used in conversation as your *end exercise* signal, and use it to dismiss the dog after training. You can use a word such as *amscray, free*, or anything else you choose—but be sure to use it consistently. When you say it, unleash the dog, sound happy, and, if necessary, toss a toy for him to chase.

Know How to Hold the Leash

The proper way to hold the leash was discussed in Chapter 7 (see "Using the Leash"), but it bears repeating: it is very important to hold the leash properly for all exercises.

All training is done on a loose leash. This does not mean that you give the dog the whole six feet of leash, but that you hold the leash

> Training a dog on a loose leash prepares the dog for off-leash work.

in a manner that does not pull on the dog's collar. If you hold the leash too tightly, the dog may learn to depend on the tension of the leash to maintain his position. Some dog trainers teach the *heel* exercise by having students hold the leash so tightly that the dog cannot move from that position. Again, this does not teach the dog where to be, but it does teach the dog to rely on the leash. By contrast, using a loose leash teaches the dog to respond even when he feels unrestrained. Training your dog in this fashion will teach him to work reliably on-leash, and prepare him to have the necessary self-control and independence for off-leash work.

The leash should always be held in your right hand. Place the loop end of the leash tightly over your right thumb, letting the leash fall over your palm, and closing your hand over the leash. Never put the loop of the leash around your wrist because if the loop is around your wrist, a dog can pull the leash out of your hand. With the loop around your thumb and the leash securely held with your hand at abdomen level, you will be in a strong enough position to prevent a dog from pulling the leash out of your hand. This is the way to hold the leash for all exercises.

Any slack in the leash can be taken up by folding the leash into your fist. In some exercises, you will give the dog all six feet of the leash. Even in these cases, you must still keep the loop over your thumb and keep your hand at abdomen level to maintain your strength.

Now that you're all set up, it's finally time to start the training exercises! The next two chapters deal with the specifics of basic and advanced obedience training.

9

Basic Obedience Training

You can start your basic obedience training as soon as your dog is comfortable wearing a collar or body harness and being on a leash. Only work on one exercise at a time. Spend about a week focused on each exercise as it will take this long for the lesson to go from the dog's short-term to long-term memory. It is unfair to the dog to rush the learning process, which sets him up for failure.

Training your dog requires you to become a teacher, and teaching a dog means that you must move correctly to *show* the dog what you want. Remember: dogs do not speak your language (see Chapter 3: Talking to Your Dog). You must handle the leash and treats correctly (see "Treats and Training" in Chapter 4, "Using the Leash" in Chapter 7, and "Know How to Hold the Leash" in Chapter 8). Maintaining consistency in your timing and movements—including when you give praise and treats, how you use facial expressions and tone of voice, and when and how you react to your dog's actions—is very important for learning. Once the dog learns how you work, you can relax your technique.

For each step in training, a certain exercise is outlined below. This includes how to use the equipment for each exercise and the proper way to move in order to maximize your dog's ability to learn. The training steps below will show you how to use your body to communicate the lessons to your dog. Note also that I have named these obedience exercises with the command words that I tend to use when teaching them. You needn't feel constrained to these words. You can use any words that work for you, so long as you have not already taught your dog another behavior using the same word.

Basic Obedience, Week by Week

The complete obedience program follows these steps after the dog is used to the equipment (see Chapter 7). Each day, your training sessions should include no more than 15 minutes of work per session, using the 5-1-5-1-5-quit Training Formula (outlined in Chapter 8). Each new lesson in the schedule will build on the previous one. Practice the old exercises and slowly add new exercises to the routine each week, as illustrated below. It should be noted, too, that this schedule is not rigid; it should be adjusted to accommodate your dog's individual learning rate. For example, some dogs may need two weeks to master a new command before you move on to the next step in the routine.

BASIC OBEDIENCE TRAINING SCHEDULE

Week 1
   New exercises: *Sit, Walk with Me*

Week 2
   Old exercises: *Sit, Walk with Me*
   New exercises: *Heel, Sit-Stay*

Week 3
   Old exercises: *Heel, Sit-Stay*
   New exercise: *Come*

Week 4
   Old exercises: *Heel, Sit-Stay, Come*
   New exercises: *Go to Heel, Down*

Week 5
   Practice all exercises with distractions

Basic Obedience Exercises

SIT

For many people, *sit* is the easiest and most basic exercise to teach. Often, it is the first thing they teach a puppy. *Sit* is best taught with a treat and/or a clicker.

At first, you want to stand in front of your dog or at the dog's side. Without saying anything, and with a treat in your hand, raise the treat over the dog's head so the dog will have to tilt his head back. When he tilts his head back far enough, his rump will go down into a sit. (You can try this for yourself: stand straight and tilt your head back as far as you can. You, too, will feel the urge to sit.) Be careful, though: if you hold the treat too high, the dog will jump for it, which is not the behavior you want to teach.

Luring the dog with a treat works with both puppies and adult dogs. However, if you have a dog that does not respond to being lured with a treat, you may have to show the dog that you want him to sit. To do this, gently put your hand under the dog's chin and tilt his head straight back. (Do not tilt his head to either side. This method only works if his head is tilted straight back, because this way he will get the same urge to sit as he would if he were lured with a treat.) As you tilt his head, gently touch his hind legs above the point of hock. He will sit. The second he does so, release his head and either give him a treat with a hearty "Good boy," or click him. This method works best if you click and treat as quickly as you can.

If your dog is clicker trained, another way to teach the *sit* command is to click your dog whenever he sits on his own. This can be done randomly throughout the day or evening. It will not take long before your dog will offer you sits to get the click and treat. Note that you must have your clicker on hand at all (or most) times to do this. If your dog sits on his own across the room, you can click him as soon as he sits. If you are using a clicker, you do not have to give him a treat right away; it is also okay, once in a while, to click the dog without a treat.

When your dog will sit reliably with the treat, you can say, "Sit," just before you use the treat to lure him into a sit. Most dogs learn this exercise quickly, but it will still usually take a few days, doing it often throughout the day, before they get the idea. When training *sit*, do the exercise two or three times in a row, then quit. You can do it throughout the house and/or on or off-leash outside. If your dog is off-leash, be sure you are in a safe area where he cannot run away.

It does not matter how your dog sits as long as he does sit. Some dogs do not like to sit straight with their hind legs directly under them. It is okay for your dog to sit to one side or the other. Give your dog the freedom to sit the way it is most comfortable for him. This is especially important if you are training an older dog, because the dog may have an injury, be arthritic, or have a hip problem. Although it is a small thing, giving your dog the freedom to decide how to sit for you helps build the bond between you and your dog and allows him to become a free-thinking dog.

If your dog outright refuses to sit in any fashion, it would be wise to have him examined by a veterinarian to rule out medical issues such as hip dysplasia or arthritis.

Finally, to avoid pattern training when teaching your dog to sit on command, teach him to sit no matter where you are in relation to him. In other words, if you want your dog to sit in all situations, do not always stand in front of your dog when giving him the command to sit. Remember, your dog only knows what you *show* him. If you are always in front of your dog, he will think that he only has to sit when you are in front of him. By telling him to sit when you are at his side or behind him, or elsewhere in relation to him, he will learn that *sit* means to sit no matter where you are. A dog must listen no matter what the situation is or what position you are in.

WALK WITH ME

The next exercise is *walk with me*. The goal of this exercise is to teach the dog to follow you, and to walk nicely without pulling. Be aware that *walk with me* is not *heel*—these are different exercises.

In *heel*, as we shall see in the next section, the dog is expected to take a specific position next to you. *Walk with me*, on the other hand, teaches the dog the concept that he has to go with you, regardless of where he is in relation to you. It is taught within the range of the six-foot leash and your arm.

Start this exercise facing your dog. When you move, you will walk backwards so that you can watch what your dog is doing and so you can make eye contact with him. Your dog is more likely to focus on you if you have eye contact.

Facing your dog, say his name, pause for a second, then say, "Walk with me." (Some people like to shorten the command to just "Walk" and that is okay.) It is important to pause after saying the dog's name and before giving the command so he does not learn to move at the sound of his name. His name is an attention-getter only, not a command.

As soon as you finish saying the command, start walking backwards while luring the dog with a treat. Take just a few steps and then stop and reward your dog with a treat. Be sure to stop and reward your dog only when he is following you and when he stands right in front of you. Do this until your dog understands that he is to follow you. It should only take a day or so.

Once your dog is following you consistently, you can walk normally. Allow your dog the full length of the leash and your arm, and let him follow you in front of, beside, or behind you, as long as he continues to follow you and does not pull when he reaches the end of the leash.

Walk with me is also an important exercise for teaching your dog that you are the leader, not him. It is important to make sure that *you* determine where and in what direction you and your dog will walk. People who allow their dogs to pull and then follow the dog are telling the dog through their body language and movement that the dog is in control. If your dog pulls—and most do!—simply repeat the *walk with me* command and immediately walk in the opposite direction than the one in which the dog wants to go. Do not jerk on the leash or scold the dog. Your attitude should be, "Oh, you weren't looking? We are going this way." As soon as the dog walks in your direction, stop and praise the dog.

Do not pull on the leash yourself. Unless the dog starts pulling, the leash should always be loose. Your dog knows the difference between you pulling and him pulling. Pulling or jerking the leash will be interpreted by your dog as punishment. Instead of pulling on the leash, I recommend using a positive teaching method: showing the dog with your body language—in this case, the direction in which you are moving—where he is supposed to go. For some dogs, this means you will be walking backwards and changing directions so often that a person passing by might think you have had too much wine to drink. So be it! That may be what it takes to teach the dog.

For dogs that are very dominant and try to bully their owners into letting them take control and go where they want to go, simply walking in another direction than the one they are trying to go in accomplishes nothing. If you have a very dominant dog, it is best to use a head harness for this exercise. This will allow you to turn the dog's head to get him to focus on you. Turning his head using the head harness will get him not only to follow you, but also to focus on you. This will help him learn the concept of *walk with me*, and, again, get him to understand that you are the leader, not him.

Some dogs may take longer to accept this concept than others, and this has a lot to do with the individual dog's age, personality, life experience, and breed. Once your dog has learned *walk with me* and will perform it reliably—usually after a week of practice—other members of the family and friends can begin to walk your dog. All other training exercises should continue to be the responsibility of the dog's one trainer.

AN EXERCISE FOR THE DOG THAT IS AFRAID
TO WALK OUTDOORS

There are a number of reasons why a dog may be afraid to walk outside. Some if it is due to a lack of proper socialization, genetics that result in a poor temperament, and sometimes the environment just seems overwhelming to the dog. This can happen with dogs that cannot tolerate the noise of an urban environment or even dogs that are afraid of the machinery and/or animals in the country.

Before you can train your dog outdoors, you need to build the dog's confidence so he can focus on training. If the case is very severe, it would be in the dog's and your best interest to consult with a certified canine behavior consultant.

However, you can try the simple method below, which works for most dogs that are afraid to walk outdoors.

STEP 1

Start by taking the dog as close as possible to the area that he is afraid of without making the dog so afraid that he runs or freezes. At that point, sit or stand with the dog calmly. If you live in a suburban or urban area, it may mean sitting quietly on your front steps at a time of day when there is little auto and pedestrian traffic. As the dog relaxes, do this for longer periods (minutes, not hours). When the dog can handle this, you can move on to Step 2.

STEP 2

Using flour, draw five circles, arranged in the pattern of a five-spot playing card. The circles do not need to be big—six-inch circles should do. To begin, draw the circles only a few feet apart (though if the dog is large, you may have to space the circles a bit farther apart). The goal is to have them spaced far enough apart that the dog must take three to five steps between each one.

With the dog at your side in *heel* position, walk to the first circle. As soon as your dog reaches the circle, praise, click, and/or treat the dog. Stop for a few seconds and then move to the next circle. The dog can smell the flour and see the circles, giving him a goal that is easy to reach. He only has to walk a short distance to get the reward. The dog then associates walking to the circle to get the reward and becomes comfortable doing that.

STEP 3
As the dog gets the idea, mix up the route you use to walk to the circles. Do not always go to them in the same pattern. Five circles give you many choices about which circle to start with and which to go to next.

STEP 4
When your dog willingly moves to each circle, it is time to make the circles farther apart. Over the course of your training sessions, keep moving the circles farther apart. By the time you get to the last step, the dog will have gotten used to walking farther and farther until his fear of walking outside is gone.

HEEL

Prior to doing the *heel* exercise, you should master *sit* and *walk with me* on command. Note, however, that during any single training session you do not want to switch back and forth between *heel* and *walk with me*. This is important because you want the dog to fully understand the difference between *heel* and *walk with me*, and this means allowing your dog to learn both concepts independently first. Once your dog knows the difference, you can switch back and forth as circumstances change.

HOLDING THE LEASH FOR THE HEEL EXERCISE

For exercises in which the dog is to walk in *heel* position, the dog sits by your left side with his shoulder even with your knee. In this position, you will need to take up the slack of the leash. To do this, loop the leash into your hand, not around it (Photo 9.1; see also Chapters 7 and 8 for further information on how to hold the leash). For *heel* specifically, take up the slack until the clip of the leash and the D-ring of the collar form a "V" (Photos 9.2 and 9.3).

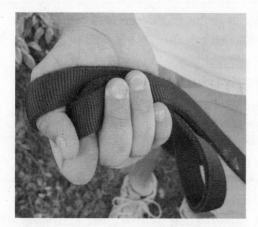

Photo 9.1 Once you have the loop around your thumb, take up the slack in the leash by looping the leash in your hand and closing your hand around the gathered leash. Only loop the leash around your thumb and never around any other fingers.

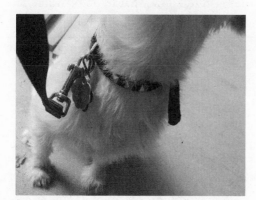

Photo 9.2 Riley demonstrates making a "V" with the leash and a buckle collar.

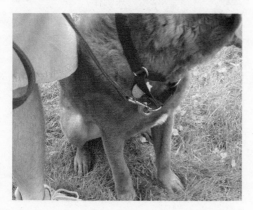

Photo 9.3 Grady demonstrates appropriate slack in the leash, forming a "V" with the leash and a martingale collar.

Your right hand should be held across your abdomen, near your naval, with your elbow bent so that your hand and arm form a right angle. By holding your hand and arm across your abdomen, you have the most strength to handle your dog should he pull or bolt.

Most people will unconsciously let more leash slide out of their hand and then raise their hand to chest height to maintain control. It is, in fact, the opposite that is accomplished. The higher you raise your hand, the less strength you have since this position extends your muscles. Moreover, holding the dog in position does not teach the dog where to be, but only serves to make him dependent on the tension of the leash to know what to do or where to be. Using a loose leash allows the dog to choose to work with you and prepares him for off-leash work.

The length of the leash required to accomplish the correct position will depend both on your dog's height and your own. If your

Photo 9.4 Matt demonstrates the correct way to hold the leash. Position your left hand, and have enough slack in the leash. Here we also see the correct *heel* position illustrated by Matt and canine Grady.

hand and leash are positioned properly, you will be able to walk your dog on a loose leash but will also be able to tighten the leash simply by raising your hand at the wrist, without losing the strength of your arm.

> Having a loose leash, or a leash with no tension, does not mean that you must let out a long stretch of leash. One inch of slack will eliminate tension but still give you control over the leash and dog.

TEACHING HEEL

The *heel* exercise is used when you do not want your dog wandering for the length of the leash as he was able to do with *walk with me*. For example, if you are walking in town on a busy sidewalk, you want your dog by your side.

Although some trainers recommend it, do not have the dog look at you when he is in *heel* position. The only place a dog should look is where he is going. This is especially critical for dogs that will be working dogs, but it is also important for the general safety of any dog.

To start the exercise, have your dog sit by your left side with his shoulder even with your knee. This is *heel* position. Say the dog's name, pause for a second (because you do not want the dog to move at the sound of his name), say "Heel," and then start walking, moving your left leg first. Starting with your left leg is important because it is the leg next to the dog and he will see and feel it move. Make sure that you walk right off and do not wait for the dog to decide that he will follow. If you wait for the dog to decide to walk with you, who is in charge? Not you! If the dog has trouble following, you can lure him with a treat to get him started. As soon as your dog walks with you, praise him.

If your dog tries to pull or go off to the side, simply turn in the opposite direction while you give the *heel* command. Do not jerk or otherwise

> Remember: when giving your dog a command, be sure to use a tone of voice that communicates that you expect him to obey, but that does not sound angry or harsh.

scold the dog, but do praise him when he goes back to the *heel* position and does not pull. When you stop, have your dog sit—a skill that should be well practiced by now.

If your dog does not sit immediately, be prepared to lure him into a sit, as described in the *sit* exercise above. Do not repeat your command or wait for your dog to sit. If you do that you are showing the dog that he can sit when *he* wants, not when *you* want.

Be sure to practice both right- and left-hand turns. When starting a left-hand turn, it helps if you can swing your right leg out so it blocks the dog's path to the right. Do *not* kick the dog; just show him that he needs to turn left.

When you know you are going to stop, make the last step with your left leg and bring your right leg in line with your left. Have the dog sit in *heel* position when you stop.

When your dog is 80 percent reliable, you can start getting him to *heel* in populated areas. Expect him to backslide a bit, especially if he is young. If your dog seems willing to obey but refuses to heel or to walk after walking for a short distance, consider that he may have an injury. If the dog is small, he may be suffering from conditions such as luxating patella. Be sure to have your veterinarian check him out.

Never force an otherwise willing dog to do physical things. This is especially true if the dog has been able to do the exercise before. Be aware that your dog's willingness to run and play may not be a reliable indicator that he is not in pain. Dogs will sometimes tolerate pain in certain exciting or fun situations that they will not tolerate in training.

Whether you practice this exercise indoors or outdoors, be sure you do not follow a pattern. An example of a pattern in the *heel* exercise would be to always stop after 20 paces, or in front of the same piece of furniture, or at a specific spot outside. Your dog will notice these things and may use them as a signal to stop. Vary the number of steps you take, the turns you make, how long you wait before you start to *heel* again, and where you practice. This will avoid pattern training.

Note, too, that patterns from training the *sit* exercise may re-emerge here. When training *heel*, if the dog tries to swing around to the front of your body every time you stop, this is likely because you did all of your early *sit* training with the dog in front of you. To correct this, just before you take your last step before you stop, use your left hand to steady the dog and show him that he has to sit by your left side. If he gets in front of you before you can do this, simply take another step forward and tighten the leash on your last step so he cannot continue forward, then guide him with your left hand. Be sure to lavishly reward him for sitting at your left side.

SIT-STAY

While teaching your dog to heel, you can introduce the *sit-stay* exercise. While it is usually best to teach one concept at a time, I've learned through my years of experience that some exercises *can* be taught together, and can help to keep the dog from getting bored with training. I have found that teaching *sit-stay* along with *heel* works for most dogs.

While walking with your dog in *heel*, come to a stop. Remember: when you are ready to stop, be sure that you stop with your left foot first, as described above. This way your dog has a few seconds to realize that you are stopping. While the dog is sitting at your left side, bring the palm of your left hand toward your dog's face, and say, "Stay." Do not hit the dog's nose or face; just make him feel as though you are blocking his way.

With your hand still in place, step forward with your *right leg*. Remember your dog has been taught to follow your left leg, so by

Photo 9.5 To give your dog
the *stay* command, put your
hand in front of the dog
without touching, as you tell
him to stay.

stepping out with your right leg first you are giving the dog a hint
that he is not meant to move. Swing around so you are facing your
dog and he cannot move forward.

At first, you will stand there for about 30 seconds. Then you
(not your dog) will return to *heel* position. Do this by touching
the top of the dog's head with a finger of your left hand so that
you can walk around the back of the dog to return to *heel* position. You will be walking around the dog's left side. Touching
the dog's head will help him understand that he is not to spin
around with you as you return to *heel* position (with your dog by
your left knee), and will teach him to hold the *stay* position even
when you move.

Photo 9.6 When you return to your dog after he stays, you want to gently touch the top of the dog's head so he does not spin around to watch you walk behind him as you go back to *heel* position. This is illustrated here by Matt and canine Grady.

As your dog gets the idea that he must hold the *sit* position, you can give the *stay* command as you move backward away from the dog, slowly letting the length of the leash out so you do not pull on the leash as you walk backwards. As you move away from the dog, your leash is still being held with your right hand, but you are sliding the leash on the palm of your upturned left hand (Photo 9.7).

Most dogs try to get up and follow you because, up to now, most of the training has been teaching the dog to follow you. By sliding the leash over your left palm, you can grab the leash and tighten it with your left hand to prevent him from getting up if he begins to move. Tighten the leash by moving your hand up and toward the dog rather than pulling the leash toward you (Photos 9.8 and 9.9). If you pull the leash toward you, the dog may think you want him to come to you, but if you can tighten the leash fast enough and catch him before he gets up and takes a step, you will teach him that he is not to move. If he is too fast and takes a step, put him

Photo 9.7 When you leave your dog in the *stay* position, continue to hold the leash with your right hand while you put the leash in the flat of your upturned left hand.

Photo 9.8 Kathy demonstrates with Riley how to lean forward and gently stop the dog from breaking the *stay*. If you can stop the dog before he fully gets up, you will show the dog that he is not to break the *stay*.

back in the *original position* where you told him to stay. Dogs are very aware of their location, and constantly use it to orient themselves. If you do not return him to his original position, the dog will think that *stay* means it is okay to creep to another spot.

Repeat the exercise until the dog stays for a few seconds. When he has remained in the same place for even a few seconds, return to the *heel* position using the method described above. Gather the slack in the leash as you do this, but be sure not to pull on the leash since your dog may think you want him to get up and come to you.

Photo 9.9 Ginger and Sunny also demonstrate how to stop your dog from breaking the *stay* command.

As soon as you are in *heel* position, take up the slack in the leash and continue to *heel* your dog. As your dog begins to get the idea of *sit-stay*, you will add time (up to a maximum of one minute) and distance (up to a maximum of the length of the six-foot leash and your arm) to the exercise. Don't make your dog sit and stay for too long. One minute is about all a dog can handle at this point in training.

If your dog decides to lie down while on a *sit-stay*, this is okay! Your dog is telling you with his body language that he is going to stay there as long as you want him to—and, after all, staying is the goal, not how he stays. I would rather have a dog decide lie down and actually stay than one who is thinking of leaving the position.

If your dog lies down and holds the down while you return to him to go to the *heel* position, do not pull him back up into a *sit* position. Rather, take your right hand and, with an upsweeping wave (from the ground up), say, "Hup!" and lure him up with a treat. When he is in a *sit* position, praise him and tell him to stay. Once the dog is sitting, you can resume your *heel* exercise.

As your dog becomes 80 percent reliable with this exercise, you can practice in more populated, busier areas, but do *not* try this exercise off-leash at this point. Many dog owners become overconfident and trust their dogs too soon. If the dog learns that he can run free off-leash, it is difficult to keep him from running free when he feels like doing it. After you have successfully worked through this obedience program and have proofed your dog against distractions, you can practice off-leash work in a safe environment.

Use the word *hup* instead of *up* to get your dog to sit up when he has been lying down. You should avoid using the word *up* since you may want to use it for other things later on.

No dog, no matter how well trained, is ever 100 percent reliable off-leash. You must keep this in mind when starting off-leash practice and training.

To avoid pattern training, it is critical that, when practicing *sit-stay*, you move away from your dog using every direction in a circle. There are 360 degrees in a circle—be sure to use at least half of them. This way your dog will learn to stay no matter where you are. If you only teach him to stay while you stand directly in front of him, he will not stay if you are not in front of him.

The duration of time for which you ask your dog to stay can also fall into the realm of pattern training. Vary the time but do not go over a minute, and keep in mind that dogs are in tune with time. When you have your dog stay for up to a minute, do not add seconds one by one, but vary the time. For example, have your dog stay for 15 seconds, then 10 seconds, then 20 seconds, then 5 seconds, and so on. This will keep your dog from getting up on his own after a minute because he knows the minute is up.

COME (OR THE *RECALL*)

Coming when called, called the *come* or *recall* exercise, is a very important behavior to teach. It can save your dog's life and keep him from running away. You should never, ever scold your dog for doing something you did not like after calling him to you. Your dog will only learn that coming to you is bad and he may not do it. Your dog will not trust you. (In fact, you should not scold your dog, *period*. It does not accomplish anything and can cause serious issues. (See "Do Not Scold Your Dog" in Chapter 3.)

> Never scold a dog if he moves toward you. He will associate being scolded with coming to you and may never come reliably, especially if you are upset when you call him. Always praise the dog for coming no matter what else he did.

By the time you get to the *recall* in your training schedule, your dog should know *heel* and *sit-stay*, and be able to hold a stay. To teach him to come on command, you want to walk to the end of your leash with your arm extended to get as far away from your dog as you can. If you are not far enough away, the dog may feel as though he is already near you, but by going as far away as your leash and arm allow, the dog will feel that he needs to move toward you to come on command.

When you are in position for the *recall* exercise, be sure that you stand straight and do not bend over to call your dog. The dog, especially if he is small, may interpret your bending over as threatening, and you will send a mixed signal to your dog: you sound happy calling him, but your body language says, "Beware."

With your dog holding a *sit-stay* at the end of your leash, say, "Come," in a tone of voice that says there is no question that he is coming. Do not use a pleading tone of voice, which the dog interprets as you saying, "Come if you feel like it." As we have seen,

Photo 9.10 Ginger demonstrates how to stand straight when you call your dog for the *recall*.

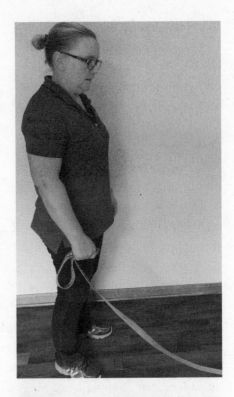

Photo 9.11 Ginger demonstrates what *not* to do when you call your dog for the *recall*. Bending over in this manner is a threatening position to some dogs and may give the dog mixed messages.

dogs can understand your tone of voice (see Chapter 3), so you should use a tone that is confident and matter-of-fact.

You may have to slap your leg with the palm of your hand to get the dog to start moving in your direction. If that does not work, use a more excited tone of voice when you say, "Come!" You can also move backward a few steps. As soon as the dog is moving toward you, return to the place you first called him. When your dog is in front of you, have him sit.

Keep in mind that the *recall* exercise might be a difficult concept for your dog, especially after having learned *sit-stay*. In *sit-stay*, you were the one who always returned to the dog, and if the dog tried to get up and come to you, he was returned to the spot where he was told to stay. We did this so the dog would learn the concept of staying where you told him to stay instead of doing what he wanted. Now, however, you are telling your dog *not* to stay where you put him, but to get up on command and come to you. To reassure the dog, as soon as he gets up and starts to move toward you, praise him in a very upbeat manner to encourage him to come.

As he comes to you, take up the slack in the leash by using your right hand to pull it through or over your left hand as you did when you returned to your dog in *sit-stay*. Again, you do not want to pull on the leash. Just take up the slack so that, if the dog should try to go anywhere other than to you, you will be able to control him.

If the dog does break, put him back in the spot where he was originally told to stay, tell him again to stay, wait about 30 seconds, and repeat the *come* exercise. You do not want to call your dog immediately or he will think that as soon as he stops, he can get up again.

As your dog reaches you, it is very important that you have him sit directly in front of you, toe-to-toe. It is too tempting for some dogs to stop out of your reach. In their zeal to come

Photo 9.12 Kathy demonstrates how to slide the leash over your upturned left hand when you first teach your dog to come when called. This way, if the dog should bolt or try to go in a different direction, you can grab the leash with both hands.

and have fun with you (after all, training should be fun for the dog and you!), they may charge to you and then run right on by if you do not teach them to stop. Some dogs even think it is great fun to body slam you. We do not want any of these behaviors, so it is key, in this case, to be specific about where the dog is to sit.

Once your dog has stopped and is sitting in front of you, pause for a few seconds and then return to *heel* position in the same manner as you did for *sit-stay*.

Unlike *sit-stay* and *heel*, it is very important to teach the *recall* on its own. Do not give a new command or begin a new exercise after your dog comes to sit in front of you, and be sure to praise your dog both when he sits in front of you and when you are back in *heel* position.

As your dog gets to be 80 percent reliable with the *come* exercise on your six-foot leash, you can start to increase the distance between you and your dog a little at a time using a longer leash. Longer training leashes typically come in lengths between 15 and 25 feet. If you do not have a longer training leash, clip your two six-foot leashes together. (You should always have a spare leash on hand!)

Do not attempt this exercise off-leash during basic training. If your feel your dog is doing very well with a longer training leash and you want to add even more distance—which is a good thing to practice!—you can purchase a length of parachute cord, which is a very strong and lightweight cord. This will be cheaper than buying a new leash and has the added benefit of being as you want it to be. I would suggest buying about 25 to 50 feet of cord. There are two ways of using parachute cord in training: 1) Buy a clip and securely tie it to one end of the cord; then tie a loop on the other end that you can clip a regular nylon leash to. The leash will make it easier on your hands to handle the cord. 2) Simply tie the loop-end of the cord around your waist. In either case, be sure that your dog cannot run the length of the cord to an area that is not safe.

> Be sure to reward your dog when he comes to you, either with praise, a click, a treat, or all three.

Vary the time the dog waits until you call him. The duration of time can easily become a type of pattern training. If you always ask him to come after the same amount of time, the dog will think that is the rule.

Once your dog comes reliably 80 percent of the time from longer distances, move on to practicing having your dog come to you while you are in different positions in relation to him. You can also mix up the pattern by having the dog come to you sometimes, and other times return to the dog yourself. These methods, too, will help avoid pattern training.

It is also a good idea, once your dog has learned the exercise well (and on a shorter leash if necessary) to begin practicing *come* in areas that are more distracting for your dog. For your dog's safety, you should prepare him the best you can to maintain control with distractions. This should be done with mild distractions at first and then with tougher distractions, to prepare him for life situations—because in real life, you will encounter all sorts of distractions, big and small. Mild distractions can be anything that your dog finds interesting or is attracted to, but that does not tempt him so much that he runs toward them. Strong distractions are those that your dog is likely to want to chase. Other animals are, for example, strong distractions for some dogs. When you begin training with strong distractions, have the distraction far enough away from you and your dog that your dog notices that it is there, but doesn't go after it. Gradually work closer until the dog can ignore the distraction even at a short distance. At some point, you may have to say, "Leave it" (see Chapter 10) to show the dog that he is not to pay attention to the distraction. In any case, remember, obedience is not simply knowing what to do, but the ability to exercise self-control. That takes practice.

GO TO HEEL

The command to return to *heel* position is "Go to heel." Up to now, after *sit-stay* or *recall*, you were the one who went back to the *heel* position. By returning to the *heel* position yourself, your dog learned to hold his stay even when you moved.

Now you will teach your dog how to return to *heel* position himself. To show the dog what to do, you have to do what I call "the dance step."

THE DANCE STEP

Remember, your dog has been taught to follow your left leg. We will use this to show him how to return to *heel* position. It is a good idea to practice the step without the dog until you feel comfortable with it.

STEP 1

Without moving your right leg, bring your left leg straight back a step and slightly behind your right leg, rotating your foot 90 degrees. Your feet will form a right angle, with your left toes at a right angle to your right heel. This position will give you stability.

STEP 2

Now practice the arm movement, which will help to guide the dog back to the *heel* position. Have your arms out in front of you. Swing both of your arms away from your body and to the left. Imagine your arms traveling along a curve, moving from in front of you, out, around, and ending by

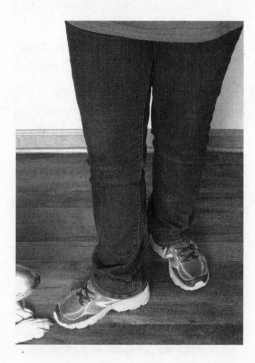

Photo 9.13 This is the correct way to place your feet when you step back for *go to heel*. By putting your left toes in line with your right heel, you do not block the dog's path as he moves back to *heel* position.

Photo 9.14 Another example of proper placement of your feet for *go to heel*. Some people have difficulty putting their foot all the way back, but as long as you have it close, it will work. The main thing is not to block the dog's path.

Photo 9.15 Matt practices the arm movement for *go to heel*, which he will use to lead the dog in a curve back to the *heel* position. The right and left hand are held together, with the leash in the right hand and a treat in the left hand.

Photo 9.16 At the same time that you swing your hands out and away from your body, take a step back with your foot. Your final position should look like the one pictured above.

your left side. Practice swinging wide and even leaning your body to the left, especially if your dog is large, so that when you introduce the dog into the movement, he will have enough room to move as well. When you practice the movement with your dog, you will hold the leash in your right hand and a treat in the left.

STEP 3
Now put the two steps together, moving your leg and arms at the same time. The moment you step back with your left leg, move your arms as you practiced in Step 2.

STEP 4
Once you have completed your dance step, bring your left foot back in line with your right. This will show your dog that he must come around to the *heel* position.

Practice the dance step without the dog first. Once you are comfortable with the movement, bring your dog into the mix. The complete exercise looks like this: the dog sits in front of you, toe-to-toe. Hold a treat in your left hand and the leash in your right hand, short enough that you have control over the dog but not so tight that you are pulling the dog. Say the dog's name, pause, then say, "Go to heel." The second the *L* in *heel* leaves your lips, do the dance step: swing your arms and your left leg at the same time so that the dog follows your left leg, making an arc away from your body. When you move the dog, you will move both of your hands and your left leg together. The right hand will hold the leash and you will use your left hand to lure the dog with a treat, if necessary. As soon as the dog is facing your left leg, bring your left leg alongside of your right leg (which has not moved). The dog will have followed your left leg, as he is used to doing, until he is in *heel* position, at which point he is to sit. The whole movement should only take a few seconds. The faster you move, the smoother the step will work.

It is important to swing your arm and, if necessary, lean your body to the left so that the dog has enough room to follow your hand and leg in a circle back to your left side and into *heel* position. If you do not swing your arms wide or put your leg behind your body, there will not be enough room for the dog to make the swing to your left side. It is also important that, when you initially tell your dog to come, he sits toe-to-toe with you, as he should after a *come*. If the dog is not seated toe-to-toe with you, it makes it more difficult for you to swing your arms and body so that the dog can move into *heel* position.

As the dog learns *go to heel*, you can gradually stop moving your leg and arm. Some dogs will learn to respond to hand signals and will eventually learn to go to heel without a verbal command when you move your hand toward your left side.

There are some common mistakes to be aware of in *go to heel*. New trainers commonly make the mistake of stepping too far out with their left foot when they begin the dance step. It is important

Photo 9.17 Once you master the movement with your hands and foot, do it with the dog. Here, Matt shows Grady that he has to leave the toe-to-toe *recall* position and go to the *heel* position. Since your dog will already know that the word *heel* means he should follow your left leg, moving the leg while teaching *go to heel* makes it easier for your dog to understand what he must do.

Photo 9.18 As Grady goes in a circle back to *heel* position, Matt brings his left foot and leg forward with Grady to show him that he must follow the leg back into *heel* position.

Photo 9.19 Grady is finally back in the correct *heel* position, sitting by Matt's left side.

Photo 9.20 In this photo Ginger demonstrates how *not* to step back with your left foot during *go to heel*. Notice how her leg extends out from her body instead of taking the position shown in Photos 9.13 and 9.14. By extending your leg away from your body, you block the dog's path, making it difficult for him to return to *heel* position.

not to do this, as doing so will block the dog's path. He will not be able to go to heel and may not move at all.

Some people like to have the dog return to *heel* position by having him leave the toe-to-toe position in front of you, go to your *right*, then go around your body, traveling behind you and into *heel* position on your left side.

This can work with very small dogs but is risky to do with larger dogs. It requires that both of your hands be behind your body in order to pass the leash from the right to left hand and avoid having the leash wrap around your body. Having your hands behind you puts you in a vulnerable position with no arm strength: if the dog were to bolt, you could be easily pulled over and possibly wind up with a dislocated shoulder. Try passing the leash from your right hand to your left behind your back, and you will see that it feels unsafe.

There are also some common behaviors that you will want to prevent in your dog. For instance, some dogs will try to shortcut *go to heel*. In some cases, this is okay, as with dogs that pivot around to heel from a toe-to-toe position without really getting up. Since the goal of the exercise is to return to heel and the dog is doing it, this doesn't need to be corrected. What you do want to avoid, though, is having your dog run to you on a recall and go directly to heel. This is generally not acceptable since it is too tempting for the dog to keep going. However, it is a judgment call on your part since some dogs can, in fact, be trusted to this extent.

And as always, it's important to avoid pattern training. Have the dog go to heel sometimes, while at other times it is you who returns to heel. Make sure you mix it up in a random pattern so the dog does not anticipate the next command.

DOWN

Many dogs do not like to do the *down* exercise. If your dog doesn't like *down*, work on this exercise separately from the other exercises until he will go down 85 percent of the time.

There are a few reasons why some dogs will not lie down, but usually it is because the dog does not feel safe. This is because the *down* position is the most vulnerable position for a dog. For this reason, be mindful of where you try to teach your dog to lie down. If you are somewhere unfamiliar or in a busy location, for example, he may not want to go down because he feels unsafe. Do not force him to do so. Instead, try only teaching *down* in areas where the dog feels comfortable and safe. Often, this means being at home. You do not have to include *down* in the regular training routine until the dog has the confidence to lie down outside of his safe area.

Another reason why a dog may refuse to lie down on command is because he is too hyper and cannot hold still. If your dog is very active, try to exercise him with play before training so he has vented some of his energy.

It is also important to consider that a dog may not want to lie down because it is painful for him to do it. You can judge this by watching your dog lie down when he does it on his own. If your dog seems to have difficulty lying down, or always does it in an unnatural way, a veterinarian visit is warranted.

With all types of dogs, you can teach *down* with clicker training. Wait until you see your dog start to lie down, then click or reward him for doing it. Although this is a "random" way to teach *down*, it does work, and soon the dog will offer you downs to get a click and/or a treat.

Pay attention to your dog. When your dog lies down with his feet under his body, it is his way of saying that he does not plan to stay there; he is ready to jump up. When you first start to teach *down*, most dogs will go down in this manner because they do not understand that they must *stay* down. It is also common for dogs that are nervous to lie down with their feet under their body. If your dog is lying down this way, be ready to correct him for getting up.

Other dogs will roll over onto their back to try and entice you to play. Often these dogs do not plan to hold the *down* position, either, so be ready to correct them. Puppies often do this because they are bored with the training and want to play.

On the other hand, if your dog lies down and rolls over to his side with his hind feet extended, he is showing you that he is prepared to stay for as long as you want. To teach your dog to be a free-thinking dog, you want to let him go down in the position that is most comfortable for him. Never correct the dog for the way he lies down, so long as it is clear he plans to stay there.

Since *down* can be a stand-alone exercise, you can practice it any time by itself, or add it into other training where appropriate. Once your dog has mastered *go to heel*, for example, you can add *down* to the exercise if your dog is comfortable going down in that training location. To do this, have your dog do a *sit-stay*. Then, standing in *heel*, transfer the leash to your left hand. (This is the

Photo 9.21 When a dog lies down with his feet to the side, such as Grady is doing in this photo, it is his way of saying that he will hold this position. If a dog's four feet are under his body, he is not likely to hold the position for more than a few seconds.

only time you put the leash in your left hand; it is important to use the same technique to hold the leash as you do with your right hand; see Chapter 8.) Next, turn and face the dog's right side so that your knees are in line with the dog's right shoulder.

Gently put your left hand (with the leash in it) on the dog's shoulder blades. You will have to bend over to do this, so it is important to stand at the dog's side and not in front of him. If you stand in front of the dog, you present yourself in a position that is potentially threatening to your dog, and you block his ability to move forward and lower himself to the ground. So, all in all, there is greater chance that the dog will go down if you stand beside rather than in front of him.

Be sure you do not put your hand on the dog's back or neck. The purpose of putting your hand on the dog's shoulder blades is *not* to push the dog down, but to prevent him from getting up. Your touch on his shoulders should, therefore, be feather light.

Photo 9.22 With a treat in his right hand and his left hand gently held on Grady's shoulders, Matt prepares to show Grady that he is to lie down.

When you are in position, take a treat and put it in front of the dog's nose. Then, as you say, "Down," lure the dog down by bringing the treat directly down and slowly out in front of the dog so he goes down and follows the treat. Generally speaking, you should bring the treat down from the dog's nose to the ground and out in front of the dog slightly so that when he follows the treat he naturally has to lie down. You will have to experiment to find the position that works best for you and your dog, but in all cases, you do not want the treat so close to the dog that he bends his head into his chest, causing him to get up, nor so far that he has to stand up to follow the treat. As soon as the dog is in a prone position, say, "Stay," and give him the treat.

This maneuver sometimes takes practice, but it is useful to do as it will begin teaching your dog a hand signal for *down*: motioning with your hand, palm down, toward the ground.

Photo 9.23 As Matt lowers the treat at the correct distance from Grady's nose, the dog goes into a *down* position. Notice that the leash is held in the left hand while doing this exercise.

DOWN-HUP *AND OTHER COMBINATIONS*

When you want your dog to come up from a prone position, use the word *hup*. (As mentioned before, *hup* may be used instead of *up* since you may want to use the word *up* for other exercises later.) You can also experiment swinging your hand, palm up, in front of the dog to give him a hand signal to rise to a sit. When your dog is 80 percent reliable, you can lengthen the distance and time you have your dog hold *down*.

Many dogs will try to get up from prone position before you tell them to. It may be necessary to hold him down by lightly touching him between the shoulder blades for a second with your left hand, but you must never push your dog into a *down* position. When you push a dog down or otherwise force him to lie down, he will not enjoy the exercise and you risk hurting him. Moreover, the dog's natural reaction to being pushed is to get up or push back. When you are ready to have your dog come up, say, "Sit" or "Hup," and let him sit up. Repeat this exercise about two or three times only. For dogs that have difficulty holding *down*, tell them to go down only as long as they can, and then give the command to "Sit" or "Hup." This way, the dog still feels that you, not he, ended the exercise. As your dog is able to hold *down*, withhold the treat a bit longer each time to show the dog that he must continue hold the *down* position. Sometimes this means lengthening the exercise in one-second increments.

As your dog holds *down* longer, leave him in the same manner as you did with *sit-stay*, gradually walking to the end of the leash and having the dog stay lying down for up to three minutes.

When you return to the dog, you will return to *heel* position as you did with *sit-stay*, say, "Hup" to have the dog sit up, and then continue heeling. In fact, *down* works well if you incorporate it with *go to heel*. Every now and then, when you command your dog to go to heel, have him lie down first and then sit. This helps to prevent pattern training and keep your dog from getting bored with the same routine in training.

You want your dog to learn to drop on command in any circumstance, no matter where he is in relation to you, so you will want to start telling your dog, "Down," at greater distances. Have your dog do a *sit-stay*, then move away from him (using all directions). At first, stop a short distance away (maybe 10 feet to start), and have your dog lie down. Gradually add distance to this.

You also want to teach your dog that he may be told to drop or lie down even while he is moving or otherwise active. Once your dog responds reliably to *down* from a stationary position, you can begin to teach him to lie down during a *recall* exercise. Have your dog do a *sit-stay*, move away from him, then tell him to come. Before he gets to you, say, "Down." Your dog will be confused at first, and you may have to get closer to him and reassure him with your "down" hand signal. When he drops down, wait a few minutes, then call him to finish the *recall* exercise. Gradually, your dog will learn to drop down on command, even if he was moving, and will wait to get up until you to call him to come.

Sometimes your dog may run too fast, making it hard to get him to drop down. One solution to this problem uses a long leash to slow the dog down. For this exercise, you will need an extra-long leash or a parachute cord. You will have to judge the length needed based on the speed your dog runs.

Loop the leash or paracord around a stable object such as a tree. Attach one end to your dog's collar and hold the other as you move away from your dog in the stay position. Call your dog. As he runs toward you (and away from the tree), use the leash like a pulley to gently slow your dog by putting a little drag on the leash. Do not pull so hard that your dog stops. As the dog slows down, say, "Down." It should only take a few tries before your dog gets the idea.

While lying down in the middle of a *recall* may not seem like a big deal to you, remember that all of your training for the *down* exercise up to this point has been while your dog is stationary. In other words, dropping or lying down while moving is a new situation for your dog that he must learn, and that means you must *show* him what you want. For this reason, you might want to use command for dropping during a recall that distinguishes it from the static *down* exercise: a different command helps show the dog that the rules for lying down are different in a different setting. You could, for instance, use the word *drop*, or any word that makes sense to you. To teach this word, use the hand signal that you developed while teaching the dog *down* and give your dog the new command (i.e., "Drop"). Once he gets the idea, you can practice having him drop while you are walking, doing something around the house, or even during play time.

This completes the steps for the basic obedience routine. When your dog can do all of the exercises reliably, practice them in as many different places as you can. Include visits to stores, malls, parks, and other outings that allow dogs to enter and/or walk by busy places. Once your dog has mastered basic obedience even in busy environments, you can move on to the other, more advanced exercises presented in Chapter 10.

10

Advanced Obedience for Safe Work, Sport, and Play

The exercises in this section are not part of basic obedience training. They are, however, valuable skills to teach any dog once he has mastered his basic obedience. Some of the exercises in this section lay the groundwork for specialized training for working dogs, and some are useful for teaching your dog manners when engaging with other people. And exercises such as *waiting at the door* help manage important safety issues.

Advanced Exercises

THIS WAY

Different commands can be used to direct a dog to go right or left. There are specific commands for certain working dogs. Sled dog trainers, for example, tend to use "Gee" to go to the right and "Haw" to go to the left. As long as you are able to associate these terms with your own right and left, sled dog commands are easy to remember because the dogs are facing the same direction you are, and their right and left are the same as yours. For those who train sheep herding dogs, the directional commands are based on the clock directions: clockwise and counterclockwise. The command to go clockwise is "Go bye" or "Come bye," and to go counterclockwise is "Way to me."

I tend to use a method that allows you to reliably communicate directions to your dog without having to think about right and left, or clockwise and counterclockwise: I simply use the command "This way!"

In reality, the *this way* exercise is just a version of *walk with me*. The main difference between *walk with me* and *this way* is that with *walk with me* the dog is already following you, whereas with *this way* he is not. In situations where the dog is not following you because he is engaged in an activity on his own, *this way* teaches him to look to you to show him how you want him to change direction.

I use this method when my dogs are working a distance away from me and I want them to go in a different direction. For example, in a bird dog quartering a field or in certain SAR situations, I can show the dog from afar how I want him to change direction to cover his search sector.

To teach *this way*, begin with your dog on-leash. Simply say, "This way," and start walking in another direction. I have found that even when a dog is in front of me, he can see or hear which way to go, but using a leash when first training this skill gives your dog the added information of the movement in the leash. By practicing this in a relaxed manner, you can walk in any direction and the dog will learn to look and listen to you for cues about which way to go. When your dog can reliably follow your direction changes on-leash, begin practicing *this way* off-leash.

Like any command, you can eventually teach your dog to respond to non-verbal cues such as, in this case, a whistle, pointing, or moving in the direction you want him to go. If using a whistle, you will want to use a specific sound for right and a different one for left (that is, if you are able to keep track of your dog's right and left). If pointing, do so with your arm extended or use a long stick. Otherwise, you can also simply move in the direction you want the dog to go. The only problem with the latter two methods is that the dog must be able to see you. In general, I have not found this to be a problem since dogs have very wide peripheral vision and they do not have to look at you directly to see the signal. There are, however, situations in which you will need to get your dog to look at you in order to show him where to go—this is where actually using the "This way" command will come in handy, as you have taught your dog that he must look to you for information about where to go. If you use a whistle, of course, sight is not a problem: the dog only needs to hear the whistle.

LOOK

Look is a handy exercise that has many uses. For SAR dogs, *look* makes it easy to show a dog where to search, or to tell the dog to look at or scent an object. In the context of assistance dogs, *look* can be linked with a name for a specific object, so long as the dog has already been taught the object's name. So, for instance, you could tell your dog, "Look for my keys," so long as you have taught your dog what *keys* means. In this case the word *look* is used to mean *find*.

The easiest way to teach this exercise is to use a tiny piece of food or a treat, putting it on the floor indoors or the ground outdoors. Point to the treat saying, "Look."

Some people worry that using treats for this exercise will teach the dog only to look for treats. Rest assured that this is not true. I have done this with many dogs and never had a problem transitioning to other objects. People also worry that using food outdoors will encourage the dog to pick up other things and eat them. I have not found this to be true, either, since you should only need to use the food a few times before the dog understands the exercise. Scientists have shown that dogs can follow our gaze as well as where we point, making this exercise easy for dogs to grasp.[1,2]

As the dog learns that *look* means he is to go look for something where you indicate, you can practice hiding the object you

Photo 10.1 Kevin is
teaching Sunny to look
where he points.

want the dog to find and directing him to the area. As you practice
this, gradually increase the distance between the object and your
dog. This way, you will be able to send your dog out to look for
something even if you are not close to the place where you want
him to look.

As you train your dog to look for specific things, he will understand that when you tell him to look, he should look for the object
that he is trained for. In the case of SAR dogs, you may train
him to look for human scent. As with the keys example above,
you can also teach your dog the names of specific objects that you
want him to find. This will tell the dog exactly what to look for.
Teaching your dog the names of objects is necessary if you plan
to cross-train your dog to find different things. For example, you
can have a word for general human scent and another word for the
scent of a specific person. And remember: as we saw with Chaser
the dog (Chapter 1), dogs are able to identify literally hundreds of
individual objects. Your dog will be able to look for as many objects

or scents as you want him to as long as you take the time to teach him the specific names of these things.

Once your dog understands the *look* exercise, begin applying it to different, increasingly specific circumstances. On the job, you want to have the ability to direct your dog to very specific search areas. In a search and rescue context, for example, a dog could be searching in thick brush and scent could be trapped in the brush "cave"—an area in the brush where the branches grow so long that they fall to the ground, closing off the area around the trunk. The dog may pass by since he cannot detect scent, but you may want the dog to go into the brush cave to search. If you've trained your dog well, and practiced *look* in diverse and specific circumstances, you will be able to command the dog to look in the brush cave by pointing into the brush.

DON'T TOUCH AND TAKE IT

Don't touch and *take it* are taught together. For your dog, *don't touch* will mean, "You can look at it, and you *may* get it, but not until I tell you to take it." *Don't touch* can thus be used to teach your dog that there are certain things he is not allowed to touch unless otherwise told, though he can be near them. An example would be if you drop something on the floor by accident: you don't want your dog to touch it, but he also doesn't have to walk away. Note that this is different from the *leave it* exercise, which is described below.

The easiest way to teach *don't touch* is this: while your dog is looking at you, put a treat in your hand, then put your hand palm down on the floor in front of him. The dog will try to get the treat that is under your hand. As the dog does this, say, "Don't touch." The second he pulls back, giving up trying to get the treat, say, "Take it," and let him take the treat. It is not unusual for the dog to scratch, lick, and paw at your hand in the beginning, but after a few attempts, he will stop. In most cases the dog will do this gently enough not to hurt you. If it is difficult to bend down and use your hand, or if your dog is too aggressive, you can place the treat under your foot. If you do this, be sure not to crush the treat by putting your foot all the way down to the floor.

As your dog gets the idea and waits while the treat is in your hand, you can say, "Don't touch," while you raise your hand, showing the dog the treat. If the dog starts to try to get the treat, cover the treat with your hand and again say, "Don't touch." Again, as soon as he gives up, say, "Take it," and let him have the treat.

Work up to the point where the dog is able to restrain himself from taking the treat even when it is lying in front of him. You can also increase the time the dog must wait before you tell him to "Take it," as well as make the treat more tempting. Remember, obedience is not a matter of knowing what to do, but the ability to exercise self-control; this lesson is perhaps best demonstrated in this exercise. By increasing temptation and time, you are allowing your dog to develop self-control.

Once your dog understands *take it* in the context of *don't touch*, you can use it to teach your dog to take other objects. This skill will

Photo 10.2 Kevin and canine Sunny demonstrate *don't touch*, which means, "You can look at it, and you *may* get it, but not until I tell you to take it."

come in handy if you want to teach your dog to pick up or bring things as part of other exercises, such as *fetch*. You can also use it to teach your dog to carry things or, in the context of SAR training, to use a bringsel—a leather strap attached to the dog's collar that he grabs and carries back to the handler as a way of alerting the handler that he has found the missing person.

GET IT AND BRING IT

Get it can be taught once the dog has learned *take it*. *Get it* is used when you want the dog to leave you in order to go and get an object. Although both *take it* and *get it* are useful for teaching *fetch*, there may also be situations in which you did not throw something for the dog to get, yet you still want him to pick up and bring an object to you; for this reason, it is useful to teach your dog the concept of *get it* independently of *fetch*.

You can practice *get it* both indoors and outdoors, so long as the area is fenced to keep the dog safe. Start with a toy that the dog loves to play with. You can tease the dog with the object to increase his drive to get it if necessary. With the dog at your side, toss it a short distance from the dog. As you throw the object, say, "Get it." Just before the dog grabs the object, say, "Take it." As he starts to bring it back to you, say, "Bring it." Some dogs do this on their own, without training. If your dog is one of these, you are merely adding a name to the action, which is perfectly fine. In every case, however, a clicker is very handy for this teaching exercise. You can give your dog a click just after he takes the object in his mouth and when he returns to you. Since the dog will not be close enough to you to get a reward, the click is a good way to let the dog know you wanted him to take the object.

If your dog runs to the object but hesitates to pick it up, you can go over to him and, pointing at the object, say, "Take it." If necessary, you can put your hand under the object as though you are going to give it to the dog to encourage him to take it.

If your dog runs to the object, takes it, but does not want to bring it back to you, try luring the dog back to you by acting playful. As soon as the dog moves in your direction, you can encourage him by giving him a click or by praising him. You can try telling your dog to come if your dog is enthusiastic about holding on to the object; however, dogs will often stop playing and drop the object when told to come because they go into a more serious training mode. If necessary, you can put your dog on a long leash and gently guide him to bring the object to you.

While it is important to keep the training upbeat, if your dog tries to tease you with the object by playing the "ha-ha you can't catch me!" game, do not laugh or respond to this behavior. You can try standing still, not engaging with the dog, or you can simply walk away, letting the dog know that the session is over. After a few minutes, you can try again, acting in an upbeat manner. This will show the dog that you will only work with him when he behaves. In every case, when your dog brings you the object, praise him lavishly.

As your dog learns *get it*, *take it*, and *bring it*, you can expand your practice by placing an object that the dog does not normally play with (I often use a hand towel) within the training area. Send the dog toward the object with a "Look" command. When he reaches the object, say, "Take it," and then, "Bring it."

Some dogs will eventually learn to put the concepts *get it*, *take it*, and *bring it* together, either by understanding them all to belong to *bring it* or by combining them in *fetch*, discussed further in Chapter 12.

OUT

Out is typically used to teach a dog to hand you an object or let you take an object from his mouth. It is often used after you teach your dog to bring you an object in order to get the dog to give the object to you. The easiest way to teach the *out* command is to make a trade: take hold of the object in his mouth while you offer him a treat and say, "Out." Do not attempt to pull the object out of the dog's mouth; when you do this, the dog's instinct is to clamp down. Instead, wait for him to open his mouth as he tries to take the treat before you take the object.

While you practice this exercise, be sure to sometimes give the object back to the dog so he does not learn that every time he gives up an object, he loses it for good. This is especially important with young puppies. While puppies will often take things you do not want them to have, if they learn that they always lose all the "fun" things, they will be unwilling to give them to you, and may start playing the "ha-ha you can't catch me" game.

Out is a very important command in some working situations. When, for example, a bird dog brings you the bird or bumper (a training device for bird dogs), you will want him to hold it only until you tell him to release it into your hand.

DROP IT

The *drop it* exercise is similar to *out* except *drop it* is typically used to have the dog spit something out without the handler actually having to take it from the dog's mouth. There may be situations in which your dog picks up something that you do not want to touch yourself, but that you want out of your dog's mouth. This could be an animal carcass, a bone, or something that is not safe for your dog to have in his mouth, such as a broken piece of plastic. *Drop it* becomes a very useful command on these occasions.

To teach *drop it*, use the same basic method as you did with *out*: while the dog has something in his mouth, trade him for a treat. Instead of taking the object from the dog, however, let it drop to the ground and then praise the dog. Do not let the dog take the object again. You can kick or push it away.

LEAVE IT: PREVENTING GAME CHASING OR "CRITTERING"

Unlike *don't touch*, where the dog may not touch an object but doesn't need to walk away from it, the *leave it* exercise teaches the dog that he may not touch or sniff an object, and that he must walk away from it and not go near it again. Furthermore, whereas in *don't touch* the dog knows he might get the object, in *leave it* the dog learns that he does not get the object at any time.

This command can be used to teach your dog not to approach specific dangers. This is particularly useful if you live in an area that has dangerous wildlife, such as snakes. Poisonous snakes or not, though, this exercise has many applications and is good for all dogs to learn. It can, for instance, be used to teach your dog not to chase your neighbor's pet cat, and it can be very helpful if you drop something that your dog should never have, such as a pill or your T-bone steak. (Once your dog has initially learned *leave it*, you can even practice dropping things on the ground on purpose and telling your dog to "Leave it." This way, your dog will learn that whatever you drop is forbidden to take.)

For this exercise you will not use any of the dog's toys or anything similar to what he is allowed to play with. Do not use food as a bait on the ground for this exercise as you did with *don't touch*. Be sure, too, that you have a bit of room to do this exercise; teaching it does not work well indoors. *Leave it* is also easier to do if you use a head harness. However, some dogs will be able to learn this exercise with a regular neck collar.

There are two levels of *leave it*: a basic and a more advanced level. For the more advanced level of this exercise, you will need a helper.

BASIC LEVEL

Start by placing an object that will arouse your dog's curiosity on a path or in a field. This could be a hat, a glove, or any other unusual object that will attract the dog's attention.

With the dog on a leash, casually start walking toward the object in the same manner that you would while taking a stroll with your dog. Watch your dog carefully; the *second* he looks at or moves toward the planted object, *immediately* back up and, in a voice that communicates danger, sternly say, "Leave it!" Be sure to back up as fast as you can, but do not try to turn around—it takes too long to do that. As soon as the dog stops looking or trying to look at the object, stop and highly praise him.

It is important that your dog not simply move away, but stop looking at the object. If your dog continues looking at the object, then he is still focused on it, and you are merely a nuisance pulling him away. He will not learn to turn away if his mind is on the object. The physical act of moving his head in your direction (by using a head harness) helps the dog understand that he must not look at or go toward the object. What you are communicating to the dog is that this is something dangerous and he must not go toward it. If you do not use a head harness, you will have to lure the dog's head around with a treat instead, trying to pull the dog gently with a neck collar.

As your dog learns *leave it* and is able to walk away from the objects that you plant in his path, you can start using objects that will be more tempting for the dog. To do this, get a piece of real or fake fur. (Fake fur can be found at sewing stores where they sell fabrics that look like fur. Real fur can be found in antique shops that sell old clothing. Removable fur collars from old coats and fur shoulder drapes work well.) Tie the fur into a ball about the size of a squirrel or small rodent and place it in the area where you will walk. When the dog tries to go toward the fur, repeat the procedure outlined above until he is capable of walking away on command. Once he can do this, he's ready for the *really* hard test.

ADVANCED LEVEL

Enlist a friend or family member to help you with this exercise. Choose a signal, such as tapping the top of your head, that you will use to communicate with your helper later on. Tie a long, lightweight string to your ball of fur, then have your helper hide out of sight and downwind from the dog. (You want the wind blowing from the dog to the person hiding so the dog will not smell your helper and associate a human hiding with this exercise.) Walk with your dog in your training area as you did before; as you approach the fur ball, use your pre-established signal to tell your helper to jerk the string so the fur jumps a few feet. (Make sure your dog does not recognize the signal to jerk the fur.) Watch your dog closely: the second he looks at the fur, proceed as you did before, using a tone of voice that strongly conveys danger to the dog as you say, "Leave it!" Move briskly away from the fur. Practice this until the dog is able to ignore the moving fur.

If you want to proof your dog against poisonous snakes or other dangerous animals where you live, you can use scent or (in the case of snakes) a dead snake or a snake skin that was shed. You could even choose to use a live snake, though if you do, be sure it is in a cage that it cannot escape from or bite through. The same rules apply for other specific dangers: use something that will allow your dog to identify what the danger is, but that will not pose a risk to your dog during training.

The amount of training it will take to teach *leave it* reliably will depend on the individual dog as well as his breed. Hunting dogs and herding dogs may find the distractions particularly hard to resist, but with persistence and patience it can be done.

WAIT

The *wait* command is a short version of the *stay* exercise learned in basic obedience training. *Wait* has many uses. You can, for example, use this when you want your dog to freeze for a few seconds in circumstances such as getting in or out of a vehicle, or going in or out of a door. It is also useful if you are walking with your dog off-leash and you see your dog approaching something that you are not sure of—for example, an abandoned well, barbed wire, or an electric fence for livestock. Your dog may not understand the dangers or avoid these things on his own, especially if he has not encountered them before. It also may not be safe in this kind of situation to call your dog to you. For these reasons, it is useful to be able to tell your dog to freeze in place. You can use *wait* to get your dog to stop until you can get near him or are able to check out the object that concerned you.

There is more than one way to teach the *wait* command. The first is this: as your dog is walking with you, give him the command *wait* and gently pull on the leash to signal that he is to stop. Have him stop only for a few seconds before telling him to go ahead again. The command for moving again can be whatever you want it to be, so long as you use it consistently. "Go" works well if you are not already using it for another command with a different purpose.

Another way to teach *wait* is to put your hand in front of your dog while the dog is moving, as you did with the *stay* exercise, and say, "Wait." When your dog stops, be sure to give him a click or a hearty "Good boy."

As your dog learns what *wait* means, you can practice it in different situations and give the command at different distances. When adding distance, be sure to do so in small increments.

DIRECTED SEND OUT

The goal of this exercise is to teach your dog to move away from you in

Teaching a dog to touch a target stick is easy with clicker training. Once the dog understands that the click means "yes," you can present the end of the target stick (or dowel) near the dog's face; when he goes to sniff it, click him. It will not take more than a few sessions for the dog to start hitting the stick with his nose for a click.

the direction that you indicate. This is easily done with clicker training, so long as your dog is trained to touch a target stick. If you haven't already, I recommend learning about clicker training from a trusted resource in order to teach this skill (see "A Note on Clicker Training" in Chapter 7).

Directed send out has several uses. It can be used to send a dog to a specific location or to teach the dog that it is okay to work at a distance from you. This helps SAR dogs that have trouble ranging far from their handlers to gain the confidence to leave their handler and go off on their own for a distance. It also helps sport and hunting dogs that have the same problem. You can, furthermore, use this exercise to send a dog out to an object, then tell him to fetch the object (Chapter 12), or to take it and bring it. *Directed send out* can be fun to use with pet dogs, as well. You can, for instance, make up games for your dog that involve going to a specific area to look for something you have hidden and getting him to find it and bring it back.

To teach a directed send out, start by getting two whiffle balls and two sticks. The sticks do not have to be fancy—they could even be branches from a tree. Place a whiffle ball on the end of each stick, making sure they stay on top of the sticks and do not slide down. Then place the sticks about six feet apart, pushing them into the ground far enough to stay upright.

Next, bring the dog (on- or off-leash) within about five feet of the sticks. As the dog goes to the ball, give him a click. A dog that is target-stick trained will usually readily go to one of the balls. However, if he doesn't, you can scent one ball with anything your dog likes. When he does head for the ball or touches it, give him a click. Then, point to the other ball and encourage the dog to touch it. The dog will quickly learn to go to each ball to get his click. Once he goes reliably to both balls, you can add commands to the exercise to tell your dog when you want him to go to the right or left stick. As usual, the actual word is not important, but it is best not to use a common word. Using "Right" or "Left" is fine, or "Gee" or "Haw" (the commands typically used for sled dogs). You could also use a word that you make up, a hand signal, or whistle if it suits your purpose.

Once your dog understands your signals for right and left, you can start to move the sticks farther apart and farther away. You can do this for whatever distance you want, even until the dog cannot see the balls. When the dog goes out a certain distance, you can also incorporate *wait* into the mix. When your dog pauses, you can then redirect him in the direction you want him to go.

Advanced training exercises are useful for both working and pet dogs to learn, and will provide an even better foundation for any more specific training you plan to do later on. You may, however, still be dealing with some problematic behaviors in your dog. The next chapter looks at correcting—or, better, preventing—common problem behaviors.

11

Exercises for Common Behavioral Challenges

Depending on your dog's temperament, background, and training history, you may have some behavioral challenges on your hands. The challenges outlined in this chapter are quite common, but with proper training early in life, they can be easily prevented. If you do have a dog that has some long-standing bad habits, the same methods can be used to correct these, but keep in mind that training will take longer.

Off and *Up*: Correcting the Problem of Jumping on People

If a dog jumps on an object or person, most people tell their dog, "Get down." But using the word *down* for this purpose will only confuse the dog and weaken the *down* command, which your dog knows from basic obedience to mean "lie in a prone position." Using the same word to mean different things will cause your dog to no longer be sure what you mean. For this reason, choose a different word for the problem of jumping on people. I like to use the word *off*.

When dogs are puppies, most people will bend over, call, and coo to the puppy, encouraging him to put his paws on your legs. Because this is what they were rewarded for doing as puppies, many dogs to continue jumping up on people after they are grown. Instead of encouraging this behavior in your puppy, you should teach him to sit for a treat. This small behavioral change on your part goes a long way toward preventing the grown dog from jumping on people. However, if your dog has already learned to jump on people, you must undo the early training of this unwanted behavior and teach the dog how to greet people without jumping instead.

Most people will instinctively push the dog down while they say, "Down." But pushing the dog may actually reward the dog's jumping behavior, since dogs view pushing as a form of play. Old training methods recommended that the person being jumped on knee the dog in the chest or step on his hind toes to teach him not to jump. This method is, however, not in line with positive training philosophy. Any method that hurts your dog is wrong and, moreover, unnecessary.

When your dog jumps on you, instead of pushing or hurting the dog, *show* your dog that he is not to jump. (If the dog jumps on another person, you will need to instruct that person on how to show this to your dog.) To show him, simply put your hands in front of your body so your elbows are against your chest and your hands are under your chin. Turn your back to the dog and say, "Off." As soon as the dog drops down, turn around and reward the dog with a click and/or a treat.

If this does not work, you can use a method that involves a head harness. For this method, you will need someone to help you. When the dog jumps on your helper, have the helper turn his back to the dog in the same manner as above. At the same time, use the head harness to gently guide the dog off the person, saying, "Off." When the dog has all four feet on the ground, click and/or treat the dog, making a fuss over him. Only do this for a few repetitions at a time, or whenever the dog jumps on a person.

Photo 11.1 The best way to show a dog that you do not want him to jump on you is to turn your back on the dog and raise your hands, as Jade is demonstrating in this photo. Do not knee the dog, push the dog, or step on his back toes to try to teach him not to jump.

You can also simply teach your dog to sit when he greets someone. To do this, carry treats with you every time you walk your dog. Each time the dog meets someone, ask the person to tell the dog to sit. Give the person a treat to give the dog when he sits.

Teaching your dog *up*—an exercise that tells your dog to jump onto an object—can help you deepen your dog's mastery of *off*. To do this, find something that the dog can be on top of, such as a log, plank, or rock. Make sure he can get good footing on the object and doesn't risk falling or sliding off. Lure the dog up onto the object with a treat while you tell him, "Up." To encourage the dog, you can pat the object onto which you want him to jump. Once he jumps onto the object, reward him. Then, after a few seconds, tell him, "Off." As soon as all four feet are on the ground, reward him for getting off the object. Dogs generally like to play this game of on and off.

Up is also a useful exercise for teaching your dog to go onto objects that are unfamiliar to him. This will help you teach your dog to do exercises for sports (such as agility) and work (such as search and rescue).

Speak and *Quiet*: Correcting Problem Barking

Many people do not want their dogs to bark unnecessarily, and owners/handlers commonly yell at their dogs to be quiet. What these owners don't realize is that yelling only makes the dog bark more, since to the dog you are barking right along with him—and if you're barking, the dog thinks he is correct for barking.

In all fairness to dogs, we have to accept that they do bark. Dogs need to bark—it is one of the ways they communicate. While teaching *quiet* is not a way to make your dog be completely quiet all of the time, you *can* teach your dog to bark less, and by repeatedly telling your dog to not bark in *specific* situations, you can also teach him not to bark at all in those particular situations. For example, if you regularly have people come to your house for meetings, and they come approximately the same time through the same door, you can teach your dog not to carry on at those times. Training the dog in this way will still allow him the freedom to bark when someone comes to the door at another time, or under other circumstances.

To teach a dog to stop barking once he has started, I use the word *quiet*. Like always, before the dog can understand this word, you must teach him what it means. When it comes to this exercise, however, you must especially keep in mind that you will not be able to do this teaching while the dog is in a high state of excitement—which is often the case when he is barking—as he will not be able to focus on you or learn the command.

To teach your dog what *quiet* means, start by teaching the dog *speak*. To do this, tease the dog with a toy or treat until he barks, then praise him and give him a treat or a click with the clicker. Most dogs will quickly catch on, soon offering to bark for you for a reward. At this point, start watching your dog for cues that he is about to bark. When you see a bark coming, tell your dog, "Speak," and then reward him for barking. When he will consistently speak on command, you can then teach him *quiet*.

QUIET

To teach *quiet*, have a tiny treat between your index finger and thumb as you tell your dog, "Speak." While he is barking, quickly put the treat by his nose as you say, "Quiet." It is impossible for a dog to sniff and bark at the same time. (It is impossible for people, too—try it!) By repeating this, your dog will learn to be quiet on command. This exercise can be a bit tricky since you must time the treat with the command so the dog does not think he is being rewarded to speak. Be sure first to tell him, "Quiet," and *then* to give him the treat. Note that you can also teach *quiet* when your dog is barking on his own without being told by offering him a treat in the same manner as above while you command, "Quiet." In this case, however, keep in mind that if he is barking in a high state of excitement, he will not stop, and he will not learn *quiet*.

Once the word *quiet* consistently gets him to stop barking, you can apply the command to other situations. Have someone try to get your dog to bark because he wants to, not because you asked him to. (I sometimes get someone to knock lightly on a wall in the next room.) Be careful, however, to choose something that will not work your dog into a frenzy. When your dog barks, say, "Quiet," and reward him when he stops barking. As he learns to be quiet on command in this type of situation, you can apply the command to more exciting situations. Know that in certain, very exciting situations, your dog may not stop barking completely; he should, however, calm down much sooner and learn to bark less.

Correcting Aggressiveness When Guests Arrive

Controlling your dog when people come to the door is one of the biggest issues that pet owners have. As a young dog matures, he may even become aggressive toward anyone who comes to the door; this is because, as the dog grows up, his natural instinct to protect also develops. (This is especially true of breeds that have been bred for protection.) The development of more aggressive behavior can become especially problematic if a dog has been explicitly encouraged to be aggressive but has not received training to use this aggression only in specific situations. This is, for instance, often the case when a large dog is purchased with the idea that he will protect his family from an intruder. In the mind of the owner, the dog is meant to bite only invaders. Without proper training, however, he may end up being aggressive to welcomed visitors, as well.

Typically, the dog's owner will hold the dog by the neck collar while the dog barks and lunges at the door, all the while telling the dog, "It's okay, good boy." As the dog becomes more aggressive or assertive, the owner becomes more fearful that the dog will bite anyone who comes to the door. The dog senses the owner's fear and becomes even more aggressive.

What this dog owner does not realize is that he has inadvertently taught his dog to be aggressive to everyone who comes to the door. By telling the dog he is good, and it is okay, as a means of trying to assure him that certain guests are welcome and not a threat, the owner rewarded the dog's behavior. The dog could tell that the owner was becoming more upset, and this upset further escalated the interaction with the dog. Never in a million years would the dog understand that *he* was causing the owners fear! He believed that anyone who comes to the door is a threat. This is a vicious circle that, if no intervention is taken, will get to the point that the dog must be locked in another room or crated anytime someone comes to the door.

The best way to solve this problem is to prevent it from becoming a problem in the first place by using the following the method early in the dog's life. However, the same method can also be used with adult dogs to control problem door behavior that has already developed.

Begin by arranging a "dog training party." Invite 10 people to your party. Set up a room away from the front door in which your guests can do a quiet activity: visit, have snacks, or watch a video. You do not want any loud music or real "partying" at your gathering as this will distract your dog.

Next, put a big bag of treats outside the front door. Place a skid-proof mat inside, in front of the door. Having a mat near the door gives the dog a reference point as to where he should be when people come to the door.

Give each guest a number from 1 to 10 on a small piece of paper. Tell them, one by one and in numerical order, to go out the back door, walk around to the front door, take a treat, and either ring the doorbell or knock on the door. Hold your dog by his leash on the skid proof mat and tell your guest to come in. The person will open the front door, enter, and stand still, completely ignoring the dog. Initially the dog may be in a frenzy. This will depend upon how old the dog is, and what his previous door behavior has been. If the dog is highly excited, he will not respond to any commands that you give him. Wait until the dog settles down, then have the person who came through the door give the dog a treat, pat him on the head, and give him a hearty "Good boy." When the person who just came through the front door returns to the party room, the next person in line should wait about three minutes, then follow the same routine.

 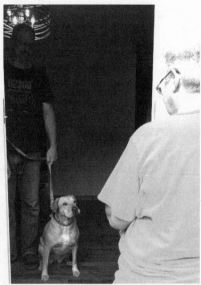

Photo 11.2 Kevin and canine Sunny demonstrate how to teach a dog to accept people who are invited to come into your home. Sunny is watching Kathy come to the door. In this scenario, Sunny is inside the home waiting to greet Kathy.

Initially, each person coming to the door will open the door himself and enter. You will have your hands full holding the dog. As the dog gets the idea and begins to be calmer when people come to the door, you can begin opening the door yourself. It is important to practice this scenario, too, so your dog will learn how to control himself not only when someone opens the door from the outside, but also when you open it from the inside.

Each person will come through the door up to 10 times. To avoid pattern training, each time someone comes into the party room, have him put his number in a bowl. When all the numbers are in the bowl, each person will take a new number and the routine will start all over again. This way the people coming to the door will arrive in a random order so the dog does not learn to expect people to arrive in a specific order.

While this is going on, you will hold your dog on the mat. There is no need to say anything to the dog. Remember that, at

first, the dog will be in a very excited
state and will not have the self-
control to obey any command that
you give him. Telling your dog to
stay, for example, would be counterproductive. However, as one person

> Remember: dogs are not capable of learning when they are in a high state of excitability. Be sure to wait until your dog calms down before rewarding him.

after another comes to the door, he will calm down, and when he
is calm he will start to learn what he is supposed to do. You can
reward him at this point. If you are using a clicker, you will click
the dog as soon as he settles down and just before the guest gives
the dog a treat.

By the time each person goes to the front door 10 times, your
dog will be very calm and will have learned to accept people at
the door. You may, however, have to repeat the training party a
few times for the dog to learn how to exercise self-control. Once
a week or every other week will work well. (Just like dogs, people
have their favorite snacks—so be sure you have great snacks for
your helpful friends!)

This positive training method is the best method to use
even if you want your dog to be a protector for the family.
What this exercise has shown your dog is that when you say
it is okay for someone to come in, or when you are there to
open the door, the person at the door is welcomed and is not
a threat. If someone were to try to enter your house when
you are not home, or to enter by means other than the door,
however, your dog will immediately recognize that this is not
normal and, if the dog has developed his protective instinct,
will protect you and your home. Not only will the dog know
that someone breaking into your home is not right, he will
also be able to smell that the invader smells different than a
welcomed guest: the scent of fear and tension on the invader
will not have been present on your guests. Therefore, this door
behavior exercise will teach your dog how to recognize the

difference between friend and foe, making your dog much safer and happier.

Wait at the Door: Correcting Bolting

A dog that tries to bolt out or in the door can be a problem. If the dog bolts out of a door into an unfenced area, the dog can run away. There is always the risk of the dog being hit by a vehicle or being stolen while running free. The best way to avoid bolting behavior is to teach the dog that he is not allowed to enter or exit a door until he is told it is okay to do so. Teaching *wait at the door* is easiest if you and your dog have already mastered *wait* (Chapter 10). You can also use *sit-stay* (Chapter 9), but *wait* is closer to what the dog will actually be asked to do.

Photo 11.3 A dog has to learn to wait at the door so you can either come in or go out without the dog bolting through the door. Here, Ginger is showing Sunny that he must wait to go through the door until he is told that he can.

Have your dog sit by the door and, for safety, have him on a leash. While holding the leash, tell him to wait or to sit and stay. Then slowly start to open the door. If the dog gets up to go out the door, close the door and give the command again. Repeat the exercise until you can open the door without your dog trying to get out.

Next, step out of the door yourself. When you are out, call your dog to come.

Be sure to practice this with all entry/exit doors in your house, both by going into the house from outside as well as going out from inside. To avoid teaching your dog that the rule only applies to the particular doors you practice with, try to find other buildings at which you can practice this behavior. This way, you will teach your dog that he cannot bolt in or out of any door, at home or otherwise.

Note, as well, that the same technique can also be used to train your dog to wait at doors inside your house or in other buildings. This can be useful if you want your dog to wait before entering certain rooms.

Correcting Problem Chewing

Puppies, like human babies, learn by putting things in their mouth. Dogs smell, taste, and feel objects with their mouths. Broadly speaking, they use their mouths the way we use our hands: it is their main means of manipulating things in their environment.

This being the case, it is important to remember that all dogs need to chew. Chewing is a natural behavior and a way for the dog to expend energy, especially if he spends the bulk of his time indoors.

Because dogs do not have hands, they use their mouths to manipulate things, to explore and learn. The mouth is a sensitive organ. Like human children, puppies, and older dogs to a lesser extent, learn by putting things in their mouth.

As was the case with barking, while it may be desirable to reduce the amount of chewing and limit the situations in which your dog chews, the goal of this exercise will not be to stop your dog from chewing altogether. Instead, you will teach him what is acceptable to chew and what is not. Ideally, this training should start when the dog is a puppy, but it can certainly be successful in older dogs as well.

As a rule of thumb, never give your puppy or adult dog old clothes to play with. This includes old slippers, shoes, and other objects such as gloves. You should also avoid toys made for dogs that resemble the things you do not want the dog to chew. There is, for example, little difference to the dog between rawhide (a leather product) and your shoes and other leather clothing. The same is true for toys made of cloth, whether they are stuffed or not. Again, there is no difference between these toys and your clothing and furniture. Toys that are made of wood are also unacceptable since some of your furniture is made from wood or has a wooden structure.

On top of that, most of the toys for dogs that are on the market are not safe for your dog. Any chew toy made of animal products, such as cow hooves, pig ears, bones, rawhide, edible chews, dental type chews, rope toys, cloth toys, and wooden objects have the potential to cause an intestinal blockage.

> If a product claims to be digestible, take a small piece and put it in water. If it does not dissolve in 5 to 10 minutes, it has the potential to block your dog's intestines.

This eliminates almost everything except Nyla-bones, Kong products, and Bite-a-Bone products, all of which are usually good choices. That being said, some aggressive chewers can destroy these products as well. In every case, you either must avoid letting them have toys that they can destroy or only let them play with their toys while you watch. If they start to destroy the toy, take it away from them.

If your puppy or dog takes something that he should not have and starts to chew it, you can trade the object for a treat and then give him an acceptable item to chew. If your dog has learned *drop it*, you can use that to get the object away from him. Never scold or punish the dog. Remember, we are teaching by showing. This means that you may have to puppy-proof your house until your puppy learns what is acceptable to chew.

As some dogs mature, they are able play with stuffed toys without destroying them. You'll have to proceed by trial and error to see if your dog is one that likes to carry, shake, and toss stuffed toys without shredding them. Some dogs cannot resist working on a toy that has a squeaker in it until they get the squeaker out. If they do this, they may eat the squeaker, which can be dangerous. The word is *caution* when introducing toys that can be dangerous to your dog.

Preventing Resource Guarding

A dog that guards his food or objects can be very dangerous. He will often attack anyone, human or animal, who comes near what he is guarding.

Some dogs seem to be predisposed to this type of behavior, but in many cases resource guarding can be prevented by proper handling and training. Resource guarding is difficult to reverse once it has become a dog's habit, so prevention and early training in this context is best. If your dog shows any signs of resource guarding, consult a certified canine behavior consultant immediately. This problem will not resolve on its own, and the dog will become more aggressive with time.

The dogs that are most likely to resource guard are those that came from environments in which they had to fight for their food. Feeding a litter of puppies from one dish of food, for example, encourages resource guarding. The puppies quickly learn as soon as they are weaned that they risk not getting enough food. Typically, the bully or the biggest puppy will get the most food. For this reason, if you are buying a puppy, make sure to ask how the puppies in the litter were fed. A good breeder will give each puppy his own bowl of food and monitor the puppies while they eat to prevent food stealing and bullying.

At home, it is easiest to prevent resource guarding while a dog is a puppy. The same technique can, however, also be successful with older dogs. The technique is this: hand-feed your puppy or dog some of the time rather than always feeding from a bowl. While your puppy or dog *is* eating from his food bowl, put your hand down to the bowl and drop in something that is better than the regular food. This way the puppy or dog learns that a hand coming toward his food bowl means good things.

The same technique can again be used to take things, such as toys, away from a dog that doesn't want to give them up. Have a special treat in your hand, offer the treat, take the toy, give the dog the treat, and return the toy.

Correcting Problem Digging

It is almost impossible to stop some dogs from digging. The time of year that dogs especially like to dig is in the spring. This is because all the scents that have been frozen in the ground thaw out. To a dog, this is a cornucopia of scent. Some dogs also find the sound of bugs or small rodents burrowing in the ground irresistible. And of course, there are some dogs that dig for the sheer joy of digging.

Some breeds, such as the Russell Terriers (and, in fact, almost all the terriers), are bred to "go to ground." For these dogs, digging is a strong instinct that they may not be able to resist.

Digging becomes an issue when a dog digs where you do not want him to. The best way to handle it is to first determine why your dog is digging. If it is from boredom, then the answer may be more exercise or more tempting toys. If the dog is a persistent digger, you can limit where he digs by designating a special, specific place where he *is* allowed to dig.

In the latter case, you can fashion a sand box–type arrangement with loose soil in it and bury treats and toys for the dog to find. When your dog starts to dig in the designated area, praise him and/or click him. If he tries to dig in other places, redirect him to his designated area. You can dissuade your dog from digging in certain areas by scenting them with household products such as vinegar. If you do this, be aware that vinegar will kill any plants growing in that area. When you don't want to kill your plants, you can try granulated dog and cat repellants that are available for purchase. Once your dog learns to avoid these areas, you should not have to use the repellant any more.

12

Tricks

Why Teach a Dog Tricks?

Tricks are fun for you and your dog, and there are even some work situations in which tricks are a huge asset. Some dogs, for example, seem to be real hams and love to perform for an audience, which is just what you want if your dog is going to be a therapy dog. People typically enjoy seeing your dog do silly tricks!

Regardless of his job, however, tricks are great for every dog to learn. Dogs are very intelligent, and life can get boring for them. Once a dog has completed his basic obedience training—and even if your dog is trained in a specialized job such as SAR—it is healthy for them to learn fun stuff to do. Tricks brighten up their days and stimulate their minds by getting them to keep learning new things. It can also help keep dogs' minds sharp as they age: scientists have shown that older dogs benefit from learning new things. It helps them have a positive attitude and slows down mental deterioration. The old saying, "You can't teach an old dog new tricks," is not true! But this is not to say that teaching tricks to an older dog is not difficult to do. Older dogs have formed habits that are deeply ingrained, and these habits may not be easy to break. But if you make the learning fun and interesting, and you approach training with lots of patience, old dogs can and do enjoy tricks.[1]

Many of the elements that you need to teach a dog tricks are based on obedience training. Remember, however, that you have taught your dog to be not only obedient, but also *free-thinking*. You should not, therefore, be too strict while teaching tricks. You don't want to stifle his creativity. Instead, and within the limits of safety, allow and encourage your dog to think and make his own decisions when working with him. That being said, always be sure to maintain control so your dog does not do anything that can cause harm or undo what you have already taught him.

If your dog comes up with a new twist to a trick, use it! Some dogs have funny mannerisms that they do automatically. These can easily be captured and trained on command by using a clicker. All you need to do is give the dog a click when you see him performing the behavior you want him to reproduce until the dog begins to offer the behavior to you for a reward. At that point, you can add a command word to the behavior that, once the dog has learned it, will act as the signal for the dog to perform the behavior. A common behavior to train by this method is spinning. Many dogs (though not all) will spin when they're happy. Simply give the dog a click when you see him spin, then add a command such as, "Spin!" As a less common example, I had a dog that was so happy she would sneeze with joy. By clicking her when she sneezed, I taught her to sneeze when I asked her, "Lily, do you have allergies?" The word *allergies* was the signal: she would sneeze about five times in response!

You should also feel free to be creative. The same technique just described can be used to teach your dog to do almost anything you can dream up, so long as you can come up with a way to show your dog what you want him to do, and reward him for doing it.

Once the dog is obedience trained, anyone, even children, can teach your dog simple tricks. I'll outline a few common tricks here. As with the obedience exercises in previous chapters, I have named these tricks with the commands that I tend to use when teaching them. Feel free, however, to use whatever commands you want, as long as they are not commands you have already taught your dog.

Above all, remember to have fun with trick training. Indeed, for many dogs and trainers, learning tricks is often the *most* fun type of training. This is usually because the attitude of the owner is more relaxed, and the dog doesn't feel any pressure. Training in this way with your dog is a great way deepen your bond.

Teaching a dog tricks is fun for both you and the dog, and helps build a positive bond. It gives the young dog something new to learn and helps keep the older dog's mind active. Because everyone smiles and laughs when a dog does tricks, it makes performing tricks fun for the dog.

The sky is *almost* the limit when it comes to teaching your dog tricks. While you can teach your dog almost anything, it is important— especially if he is an older dog—that you keep his physical limitations in mind. Be sure that the tricks do not cause pain or discomfort.

Simple Tricks

SHAKE

Shake is one of the easiest tricks to teach a dog. Have your dog sit in front of you. As you say, "Shake," take his paw in your hand and hold it for a second. As you are holding his paw, praise, click, and/ or treat him. Once the dog gets the idea, you can tell him to give you the other paw by repeating the exercise, using a different word and taking the other paw.

Photo 12.1 Kevin is
demonstrating how Sunny
can shake or "give a paw" on
command.

BANG

Bang is a variation of the trick *play dead*. The goal of this exercise
is to have your dog fall over and lie still. Start by telling your dog
to lie down. Your dog will go down to one side or the other. (If he
does not lean to one side, you can gently guide him to one side.)
Guide him to roll over on the side that he is leaning toward as you
say, "Bang!" Once he is on his side, reward him. Then tell him to
get up. With practice, your dog will begin to lie down and roll onto
his side when you say, "Bang." Once he is reliable, start pointing
your finger at him while you say, "Bang." Soon, he will fall over and
"play dead" with just the use of the hand signal.

SAY YOUR PRAYERS

Put your dog in a *sit-stay*. Using either your knees or an object
that your dog can put his paws on comfortably while he is sitting, gently put his paws on the object. Hold them there with one
hand. With your other hand, lure your dog's head between his

paws using a treat. As he puts his head between his paws, tell him, "Say your prayers." When his head is down, give him the treat. Gradually increase the time he leaves his head between his paws. The trick only needs to last a few seconds.

Soon, when you say, "Say your prayers," your dog will go to the object you used (or your knees), put his paws up, and lower his head between them.

SIT UP

Dogs tend to enjoy doing *sit up*. In fact, many dogs teach themselves how to do it. All the better for you if they do! Then, all you have to do is add a command to the spontaneous behavior using the method described above. If a dog does not do *sit up* on his own, however, you may teach it to him. This trick is easier for smaller dogs than for larger ones, since smaller dogs have shorter backs and are able to balance more easily. A large dog is, however, still entirely capable of learning this trick.

Start by having your dog sit in front of you. It helps if your dog sits squarely on his rump since he can balance better this way. While your dog is sitting, say, "Sit up," as you slowly raise a treat over his nose so that he has to rise up to get it. When he reaches the point where he lifts his front paws off the ground, you can reward him with the treat. This method will take patience on your part because your dog may try to jump up for the treat. Be sure to only give him the treat when he *sits* up.

If your dog is larger, you can try sitting him in the corner of a room with his back against the wall to help him learn to balance. You can also raise his paws for him so he sits up the way you want. Remember, you must show, not just tell, your dog what you want.

HOLD IT: BALANCING OBJECTS ON THE NOSE

This trick can be used to have the dog balance a treat or object on his nose and then flip it in the air to catch it. To start, use a treat that is flat and large enough for the dog to flip but not so big that it is awkward for him to hold. While you gently hold the dog's snout underneath his nose, place the treat on the tip of the dog's nose while saying, "Hold it." Make sure you ask your dog to hold the treat only as long as the dog can restrain himself from getting the treat. This will teach him to balance the treat on his nose. As you let go of the dog's snout, tell him, "Take it." Your dog should lift his snout to get the treat, and in doing so will flip the treat in the air. As he gets the idea, you will stop holding his snout, telling him to hold the treat until you say, "Take it."

Many people have already taught their dog to catch a treat simply by tossing treats to him, so catching the treat in this new context will likely be an easy concept for your dog to grasp. If the treat is too light or small, however, the dog may flip it behind him and not be able to catch it. You must, therefore, experiment with different treats to see which ones work best. This will depend on the size and strength of your dog.

Eventually, you can teach your dog to balance other things on his nose as well. To teach your dog to balance an object on his nose, use the same technique, holding his snout to show him that he is to keep the object on his snout until you tell him to take it or even drop it. In all cases, make sure the object is a good size for your dog and comfortable for him to hold on his nose.

CRAWL

Typically, once your dog gets the idea of *crawl*, he will love to crawl under things. It will be an adventure for him. This is especially true of terrier breeds that are bred to go to ground, and for whom crawling is a natural behavior. Once your dog knows how to crawl on command, it is a great trick to use in a routine—for instance, one in which you want your dog to sneak up on someone.

To teach *crawl*, start with your dog on a leash. Then, extend your leg out so the dog must crawl under it. Lure your dog under your leg with a treat, saying, "Crawl," while he is crouched.

If your dog is too small or too big, you might have to use a different obstacle that will be the appropriate size to get him to crawl to get under it. You can, for example, arrange cushions from a couch or chair to form a tunnel for the dog. Show the dog the makeshift tunnel and guide him under it with the leash and a treat. As with the previous method, say, "Crawl," while your dog is crouched.

As your dog associates the command with the action, you can tell him to crawl without a tunnel or your hand to guide him. The purpose of the tunnel is only to show the dog that he must crouch. To transition the dog away from using a tunnel, you may have to hold your hand over the dog's head to show him that you want him to crouch and crawl.

FETCH

Fetch is a combination of the advanced exercises *take it* and *bring it*, learned in Chapter 10. The complete *fetch* exercise involves tossing an object, the dog getting it, bringing it back to you, and either dropping it at your feet or holding it until you say, "Out" or "Drop it."

You can teach *fetch* as a one-word command after the dog can reliably get and bring an object to you. To do this, toss the object and say, "Fetch." When he returns to you, praise him lavishly. To avoid the "ha-ha you can't catch me" game, have the dog sit in front of you with the object and tell him, "Out" (again, learned in Chapter 10.) Note that if you are teaching a young dog that is not physically mature, you should only have him carry light objects. Researchers have found that if a puppy carries objects that are too heavy, it can damage his front legs.[2]

Most dogs love to play fetch and learn to do it naturally. For these dogs, you will either never have to tell them to fetch, or you will be able to quickly stop using the command. Just tossing the object for them will be enough to start the game, though typically they will at least need to see you throw the object before they fetch it.

If your dog does not learn *fetch* naturally, it is easy to teach him. Start with your dog on a leash. Toss an object or toy that your dog likes a few feet away and encourage him to get it. Once he goes by the object, say, "Take it," and then, "Bring it." When he brings the object back, you can tell him to drop it or just have him sit.

As you practice the routine, he will learn to combine all the steps together, eventually bringing the object back every time you throw it without you having to tell him. Once he does this, you can toss the object saying, "Fetch." He will soon associate the word with the routine and learn that *fetch* means to get the object and bring it back to you.

While teaching *fetch*, do not play tug-of-war with the dog or allow the dog to play the "ha-ha you can't catch me" game. If you want to play those games with your dog, use a different object or command at a different time. Since most dogs do love to fetch, they will learn the difference between these games quickly. There are, however, some breeds and individual dogs that do not like to fetch things. If this is your dog, don't force him to learn *fetch*. Teach him something that he likes instead.

> Remember: tricks are supposed to be fun for you *and* for your dog. If your dog doesn't like doing a certain trick, teach him something he does like.

JUMP THROUGH THE HOOP

For this exercise you can use a hula hoop, form a circle with your arms, or have a helper form an arm circle. When first beginning, it is easier to use a helper or a hula hoop. This is because the hoop or circle will, at first, be placed on the ground, and because you will need a free hand with which to teach the dog.

Start by holding the hoop upright on the ground. Lure your dog through the hoop with a treat as you say, "Through the hoop." At the beginning, you may have to use a leash to guide him. Be sure to have your dog go through the hoop from both directions.

Once your dog is comfortable going through the hoop on the ground, raise it slightly so he has to step up and through it. As your dog gets comfortable with this, continue to raise the hoop incrementally. Be sure to keep in mind how high your dog can jump as you continue to raise the hoop for your dog: it should always be at a height that is comfortable for your dog to jump through. As your dog gets the idea, he can begin to work off-leash.

When your dog is happy about jumping through the hoop, you are ready to add some drama to the trick. Get some thin tissue paper that people typically use to line gift boxes. Tape strips of tissue paper around the hoop so that the opening of the hoop is square. You want most of the hoop open.

Photo 12.2 To teach a dog to jump through a paper hoop, start by teaching him to jump through a hoop without paper. Then, add tissue paper around the sides of the hoop.

Photo 12.3 Riley is waiting for the command to jump through the hoop.

Command your dog to jump through the paper-lined hoop. As he gets the idea, make the opening in the hoop smaller and smaller so your dog must break the tissue paper to get through the hoop. Once your dog understands that the paper will break, you can work up to the point where he will jump through the paper while it completely covers the hoop. At that point, for show, you can use fancier tissue paper, such as one that has small sparkles in it. Like the other tricks in this section, dogs typically love doing this exercise.

Creating Routines with Reverse Chaining

If you want to teach your dog to do a routine in which you string exercises together, you will be most successful if you use reverse chaining. Reverse chaining is a method in which you begin by training the end of the routine and work back to the beginning. Because we cannot explain to the dog what the finished routine will be, if you start at the beginning of the routine the dog will have no idea how it will end or even that there are future steps in the routine. Starting at the end, however, lets the dog know what the goal is, and as the training progresses, he will be able to visualize the complete routine and understand what comes next.

So, for example, you want your dog to run into a room, jump on a bench, go under a chair, and then sit in front of you. Assuming that you have taught the dog how to do each step in the routine separately, start with the dog sitting in front of you. Then, have the dog go under the chair before coming to sit in front of you. Once he understands this, you would have him jump on the bench, then go under the chair, and then come and sit in front of you. Finally, once he can perform those three steps, have him wait outside the room. When you call him in to perform his routine, he will jump on the bench, go under the chair, and then sit in front of you.

Finally, you can teach the dog a name or signal for the whole routine. Giving the whole routine a specific name is easy to do. In this case, you could add a new word to the signal that you already use to call the dog into the room. Eventually, you will be able to use the signal alone to have the dog perform his routine.

No matter what tricks you teach your dog, remember that tricks are fun, and all dogs benefit from fun training. Many dogs spend the whole day at home alone while you are working at a job, or even attending to daily chores. During this time, your dog has nothing to occupy his mind, and this makes the time you *do* spend doing obedience training and tricks extra special to him. Moreover, for dogs with jobs, such as SAR or other detection dogs, the stress level can be high while on the job. Yes, they love doing their job, but they can also feel the tension and stress of the handler, and this puts their work on a different level than the fun stuff. Just as people need to relax and enjoy some fun activities after work, dogs need fun time, too. Be sure to give it to them, and to yourself, too!

Conclusion

The goal of this book is not to offer an intensive training program to produce award-winning competition dogs. It is to offer a program based in a positive training philosophy that will build a strong relationship between you and your dog—one that cultivates both free thought and reliability. The methods in this book are geared specifically toward the working dog handler who needs his dog to think on his own in various situations that cannot be duplicated in training. It is, however, a good basic training guide for any dog owner who wants a well-trained and happy companion.

Whatever the context, training your dog is one of the most important things you must do with your dog. Some dogs seem to learn things on their own, while others must be taught, but this has more to do with personality than intelligence. A dog can learn to do almost anything if you have the patience to teach them. In every situation, keep in mind some of the golden rules of this book: *show* your dog what to do. Take the time to teach him specific words and commands, and build a vocabulary that is meaningful to both of you. Remember that obedience is about self-control, and not just about knowing what to do.

Remember, too, that your dog will like some things, and won't like others; he'll be comfortable here, but not there. Pay attention to these things, and allow your dog to make choices for himself, remembering that if you must teach you dog to tolerate something he doesn't like—a bath, for instance—this can be done with patience and compassion, rather than force. Make sure to balance out this kind of training, and any kind of serious or specialized training or work, with some fun activities, such as doing tricks together. For your sake as well as your dog's, make sure training isn't just work!

Finally, remember that training is an ongoing process. Following this training program and the other tips in this book should give you and your dog the foundation upon which you can truly work *together*. Good luck!

Photo Gallery

The following collection of photos are some of the dogs, cats and birds that have shared my life with me. Each one taught me valuable lessons about animals. As a youth I also rode horses and they too taught me many things. I hope you enjoy seeing some of my animal friends.

Dempsey (Rottweiler), the family protector

Riley (Parsons Russell Terrier), pet and varmint hunter

Woodie (Border Collie), sheep herding and SAR dog from Border Collie Rescue

Bonnie (Turkish Angora), adopted from the veterinarian

Lily (Havanese), toxic mold detection dog featured featured on National Geographic's show *Dogs with Jobs*

Jib (Border Collie), SAR dog (all disciplines) and trained to detect toxic mold

Gus (Border Collie), adopted SAR dog (all disciplines)

Pluskat (Domestic Shorthair), pet adopted from a shelter

Sue and Puff, one of her first cats

Sparky (Beagle mix), trick
dog from Sue's early dog
training career

Mimi, (Domestic Shorthair),
adopted from a shelter.

Brat (Siberian Husky),
sled, obedience, and
conformation dog

Travis (Russian Wolfhound/
Borzoi), pet adopted from
a shelter

Thor (Doberman Pinscher),
conformation show,
personal protection,
criminal apprehension, and
drug detection dog

Baby (Domestic Shorthair),
rescued from a shelter

Mitzi (Domestic Shorthaired), found homeless on the street

Ness (Border Collie), first Border Collie to do SAR work (all disciplines) in the United States

Babs (Border Collie), pet

Scout (Beauceron), sheep herder, dual champion in conformation, and first Beauceron to do SAR work (all disciplines) in the United States

Travis (Siberian Husky), sled, obedience, and show dog

Sunshine (budgie), trained to do tricks

Notes

NOTES TO CHAPTER 1

1 American Association for the Advancement of Science, "Dogs understand both vocabulary and intonation of human speech," *ScienceDaily* (August 29, 2017), www.sciencedaily.com/releases/2016/08/160829192701.htm.

2 Springer, "Empathetic dogs lend a helping paw: Study shows that dogs that remain calm and show empathy during their owner's distress help out faster," *ScienceDaily* (July 24, 2018), https://www.sciencedaily.com/releases/2018/07/180724105921.htm.

3 University of Helsinki, "How dogs see your emotions: Dogs view facial expressions differently," *Science Daily* (January 19, 2016), www.sciencedaily.com/releases /2016/01/160119074313.htm.

4 Springer, "Dogs understand what's written all over your face," *ScienceDaily* (June 20, 2018), www.sciencedaily.com/releases/2018/06/180620125955.htm.

5 Emory Health Sciences, "Scientists chase mystery of how dogs process words: New study focuses on the brain mechanisms dogs use to differentiate between words," *ScienceDaily* (October 15, 2018), www.sciencedaily.com/releases/2018/10 /181015120901.htm.

NOTE TO CHAPTER 2

1 Edwin Hautenville Richardson and Mrs. Richardson, *Fifty Years with Dogs* (London: Hutchinson & Co., 1950). See also Richardson, *War, Police and Watch Dogs* (Edinburgh and London: William Blackwood and Sons, 1910); Richardson, *Watch-Dogs: Their Training and Management* (London: Hutchinson & Co., 1924); and Richardson, *Forty Years with Dogs* (Philadelphia: David McKay Company, 1930).

NOTES TO CHAPTER 3

1 Springer, "Dogs understand what's written all over your face."

2 Emory Health Sciences, "Dogs process faces in specialized brain area, study reveals: Face-selective region has been identified in the temporal cortex of dogs," *ScienceDaily* (August 4, 2015), www.sciencedaily.com/releases/2015/08/150804073709.htm.

3 A great at home study is "What is My Dog Saying?" by Carol E. Byrnes, found at http:// www.diamondsintheruff.com/what-is-my-powerpoint-series-on-cd. This is a power point presentation. You can also get an excellent video, "The Language of Dogs," by Sara Kalnajs, at https://www.bluedogtraining.com/videos-dvds.html.

4 American Association for the Advancement of Science, "Dogs understand both vocabulary and intonation."

5 Stanley Coren, "How to make your dog laugh (really): Humans can imitate the sounds of dog laughter. Here's how!" *Modern Dog: The Lifestyle Magazine for Modern Dogs and Their Companions* (June 21, 2017), https://moderndogmagazine.com/articles/how-make-your-dog-laugh-really/103889.

NOTES TO CHAPTER 4

1 Dog Food Advisor (https://www.dogfoodadvisor.com/) is a great resource for researching food quality.

2 Deva Khalsa, "Top foods for preventing cancer in dogs," *Dogs Naturally* (Accessed October, 2018), http://www.dogsnaturallymagazine.com/top-foods-for-preventing-cancer-in-dogs/.

3 Caroline Colie, "Can dogs eat wheat and other grains?" *American Kennel Club* (May 19, 2016), https://www.akc.org/expert-advice/nutrition/natural-foods/can-dogs-eat-wheat/.

4 American Veterinarian Editorial Staff, "FDA warns of possible link between grain-free foods and heart disease," *American Veterinarian* (July 12, 2018), https://www.americanveterinarian.com/news/fda-warns-of-possible-link-between-grainfree-dog-foods-and-heart-disease.

NOTES TO CHAPTER 6

1 University of Veterinary Medicine—Vienna, "Risk to small children from family dog often underestimated," *ScienceDaily* (September 7, 2016), www.sciencedaily.com/releases/2016/09/160907095453.htm.

2 "Dentistry," Tyler Animal Clinic, accessed October 2018, http://www.tyleranimalclinic.com/dentistry.pml.

3 "How to clip dog nails," PetMed, accessed October 2018, https://www.petmd.com/dog/grooming/evr_dg_how_to_trim_a_dogs_toenails.

NOTE TO CHAPTER 7

1 Mikkel Becker, "Head halters: The device, the uses, and the controversy," *VetStreet* (April 22, 2014), http://www.vetstreet.com/our-pet-experts/head-halters-the-device-the-uses-and-the-controversy.

2 Karen Pryor, *Getting Started: Clicker Training for Dogs* (Waltham, MA: Sunshine Books, 2005).

3 "Clicker Training Basics | 7 Insanely Actionable Steps," Wiley Pup, https://www.wileypup.com/clicker-training/. This is a great home-study for clicker training.

NOTES TO CHAPTER 10

1 University of Veterinary Medicine—Vienna, "What are you looking at? Dogs are able to follow human gaze," *ScienceDaily* (June 12, 2015), www.sciencedaily.com/releases/2015/06/150612091146.htm.

2 Public Library of Science, "Dogs succeed while chimps fail at following finger pointing: Chimpanzees have difficulty identifying object of interest based on gestures," *ScienceDaily* (February 8, 2012), www.sciencedaily.com/releases/2012/02/120208180251.htm.

NOTES TO CHAPTER 12

1 University of Veterinary Medicine—Vienna, "Brain training for old dogs: Could touchscreen games become the Sudoku of man's best friend?" *ScienceDaily* (February 7, 2018), www.sciencedaily.com/releases/2018/02/180207102219.htm.

2 University of Veterinary Medicine—Vienna, "'Bring it back,' but within bounds: Retrieval strains the forelimbs of dogs," *ScienceDaily* (January 18, 2017), www.sciencedaily.com/releases/2017/01/170118082430.htm.

About the Author

Susan and her husband, Larry Bulanda—each with over 20 years in the field—have formed and run two K9 SAR units. They formed Coventry Canine Search and Rescue, and then, when many of their missions involved the local fire department's dive squad, they joined Phoenixville Fire Department, creating and managing the K9 division, Phoenixville FDK9SAR, in Pennsylvania.

Susan started her career as a dog trainer when she was very young, and by the time she entered high school had established a business training dogs. She was recognized locally for her accomplishments by 1963 and went on to specialize in problem dogs, experimenting with ways to train dogs using positive reinforcement. She earned a bachelor of arts in psychology and a master of arts in education.

In her career, she has trained dogs for hunting, personal protection, drug detection, sled-dog racing (she owned a team of Siberian huskies), trick dog training, and SAR. She is a Certified Animal Behavior Consultant with the International Association of Animal Behavior Consultants (IAABC).

Susan was an adjunct professor for Kutztown University and is an adjunct professor for Carroll Community College, where she teaches courses on dog and cat behavior.

She is a retired senior conformation judge for the United Kennel Club, was awarded the George Washington Medal of Honor for SAR work, and holds a patent for the training and use of toxic mold detection dogs. Twice she was a judge for England's SAR competitions and has written nine books, some of which have won national awards. Her most recent book, *K9 Search and Rescue Troubleshooting: Practical Solutions to Common Search Dog Training Problems* (Brush Education, 2017) has been a big hit worldwide.

Susan was also instrumental in forming the North American Beauceron Club and is a founding member and newsletter contributor for the National Search Dog Alliance. She continues to help SAR dog handlers worldwide with their training issues.

In the corporate world, Susan was a systems analyst specializing in critical methodologies, production, and material control.

Follow her blog at sbulandablog.com and check out her website at www.sbulanda.com. She also posts on Twitter @suebpets and has a Facebook page.